TALES FROM THE SHED
AN ANTHOLOGY OF STORIES AND ARTICLES ABOUT CHELSEA FC

edited by
MARK WORRALL

TALES FROM THE SHED
An anthology of stories and articles about Chelsea FC
Copyright Mark Worrall et al. 2022
ISBN: 9798423733186
THE MORAL RIGHT OF THE AUTHORS HAS BEEN ASSERTED
Apart from any fair dealing for the purposes of research or private study, or criticism or review, as permitted under the Copyright, Designs and Patents Act 1988, this publication may only be reproduced, stored or transmitted, in any means, with the prior permission in writing of Gate 17, or in the case of reprographic reproduction in accordance with the terms of licenses issued by the Copyright Licensing Agency. Enquiries concerning reproduction outside those terms should be sent to the publishers. Email enquiries@gate17.co.uk.

Typesetting and design: Mark Worrall
Front cover artwork: Ray Wilkins 77 by Richard Schaller
Rear cover artwork: Peter Osgood 73 by Richard Schaller
www.gate17books.co.uk

CONTENTS

EDITOR'S NOTE AND ACKNOWLEDGEMENTS 1
FOLLOW YOUR HEART AND YOUR MIND WILL CREATE – MARK MEEHAN 7
JIM REEVES AND BLUE SUBMARINES – TIM ROLLS 11
A JOCK'S LIFE – CAMMY McHARG 15
AZUL ES EL COLOR! – 'SPANISH' KEN TURNER 19
WHY I CHOSE THE SHED – ROWANNE WESTHENRY 23
THE NIGHT THE LIGHTS WENT OUT – VINCE COOPER 26
GLORY HUNTER – KRAIG DIXON 30
THE SHEPHERD'S BUSH MALDINI – KELVIN BARKER 35
CHELSEA DOWN UNDER – ROSS-JOHN BONACCORSI 39
MY FAVOURITE YEAR – NEIL FITZSIMON 44
THE SHED AND ME – CLIFF AUGER 49
BACK TO THE KING'S ROAD – DANIEL CHILDS 52
PRICEY BUT NICE – CLAYTON BEERMAN 55
BUYING A MAC FOR MOSCOW – JASON GIBBINS 59
THE PLAYERS' LIFTS LEAGUE – DAVID JOHNSTONE 64
FUTURE LEGENDS – JOHN KING 67
BEST DAYS OF OUR LIVES – MARTIN KNIGHT 71
SATURDAYS KIDS – MARK MEEHAN 75
CHELSEA IN AMERICA – BETH WILD 79
YOUR CHELSEA MASCOT IS – CHRIS WRIGHT 83
BEST FOOTBALL FRIEND – RICK GLANVILL 86
CHELSEA'S DEBT TO JOHN NEAL – GARY THACKER 90
WORK EXPERIENCE – CHELSEA CHADDER 95
SILVERWARE BLUES – NEIL SMITH 98
WORLD CHAMPIONS – CHRIS AXON 102
HOME IS WHERE THE HEART IS – DAVID CHIDGEY 107
PERFECT MATCH – PAUL RADCLIFFE 111
SAME PLACE, DIFFERENT STADIUM – CHARLES ROSE 115
THE NOSE KNOWS – WALTER OTTON 119
AWAYDAY BLUES – RICHARD SCHALLER 122
BLUE PYJAMAS AND RED SQUARE – IAIN RODGER 126
STAND UP, SIT DOWN – JONATHAN KYDD 129
THE ONLY TEAM IN LONDON (TWICE) – ALEXANDRA CHURCHILL 132
THANK YOU, MR MEEHAN – MARK WORRALL 135

EDITOR'S NOTE AND ACKNOWLEDGEMENTS

Saturday, January 8, 2022

Chelsea are at home to Chesterfield in the FA Cup and I'm sat on the rattler from Cheam to Clapham Junction and as we chug through Balham Station without stopping I'm looking out of the window and my eyes settle on the sad sight of a dishevelled-looking man shuffling slowly along the platform with a dirty, torn sleeping bag over his shoulder. I wonder what his life-story is and what brought him to this point of crisis. This triggers thoughts about the forthcoming 'Big Stamford Bridge Sleep Out' fundraiser for Stoll, the leading provider of supported housing for vulnerable veterans, and the idea for 'Tales From The Shed' comes to my mind as a way of increasing awareness and raising additional funds.

I message Mark Meehan, founder and coordinator of the 'Sleep Out', and David 'Stamford Chidge' Chidgey of 'Chelsea Fancast' fame who'd broadcast a live feature during previous sleep outs in which he'd read extracts from Chelsea books and called it 'Tales From The Shed' to get their opinions. Both say it's a terrific idea so I have a think about who I could ask to write an article/story for the book. Time is tight, this year's sleep out in on March 26. I make a list of my favourite Chelsea authors, fanzine writers, bloggers and people whose dedication and support for the Club I find extraordinary and start putting some feelers out. The response amazes me!

In alphabetical order I would like to thank the following people for taking the time and trouble to write an article for this book.

Chris Axon, Cliff Auger, Kelvin Barker, Clayton Beerman, RJ Bonaccorsi, Chelsea Chadder, David Chidgey, Daniel Childs, Alexandra Churchill, Vince Cooper, Kraig Dixon, Neil Fitzsimon, Jason Gibbins, Rick Glanvill, David Johnstone, John King, Martin Knight, Jonathan Kydd, Cammy McHarg, Mark Meehan, Walter Otton, Paul Radcliffe, Iain Rodger, Tim Rolls, Charloc Rose, Richard Schaller, Neil Smith, Gary Thacker, Ken Turner, Rowanne Westhenry, Beth Wild, Chris Wright.

Saturday, March 5, 2022

Exactly eight weeks after that initial idea, 'Tales From The Shed' is published. Thank you for buying this copy and helping a worthy cause.

Mark Worrall
London, 2022

"Follow your heart and your mind will create."

Ray Wilkins

"Chelsea: It's a name. It's probably the greatest name in the world.
Chelsea: You think about it. What does it conjure up?
It conjures up the best part of the biggest city in the world.
It's magical."

Jimmy Greaves

"FOLLOW YOUR HEART AND YOUR MIND WILL CREATE"
The story behind the 'Big Stamford Bridge Sleep Out'.
Mark Meehan

April 5, 2018

I am still reeling from the kick in the guts yesterday brought me. I am on a few days leave from work as need to paint the house and news came through the day before that one of my early Chelsea heroes Ray Wilkins has passed away.

24-hours later it was still hard to take in. Just reading Ray's last text message to me left me with a lump in my throat and a tear in my eye and today was no better. So what can you do? I had tuned into 'talkSport', a stable home for Ray as a football pundit, and listened to former 'talkSport' colleagues Jim White, Simon Jordan and Alan Brazil as they hosted their regular morning show and asked listeners to ring him with their memories of Ray.

Then mid-morning an anonymous ex-soldier from Cardiff rings into Jim White's show and tells his tale to the many listeners about how when he was homeless and sitting on the floor outside West Brompton Station, Ray came over and sat down with him and shared his bit of cardboard.

"He took the time to sit and talk and we were chatting about the army. We were sat chatting and he gave me £20 and told me to get myself a hot meal and then he took me across the road to buy me a coffee.

That night I took that £20 and I got some shelter and a hot meal. During that time when I was in the shelter. I met a guy who was helping ex-soldiers who put me in touch with decent people who would help me. I am now fully recovered. I'm not gambling. I have my own place, a beautiful girlfriend who I am about to marry and I put it down to the time that Ray took to give to a man that was nothing to him, and a stranger, and I am sorry if I'm getting emotional, but he was a real, real hero to me and millions of others across the world."

It was a very moving phone call that clearly knocked everyone back in the 'talkSport' studio. Even listening back four-years later you can hear the emotion in the caller's voice. Very, very moving.

January 8, 2022

Four-years later and pre-Chelsea's FA Cup tie against Chesterfield, Mark (Marco) Worrall asked me how did the 'Big Stamford Bridge Sleep Out' come about and where did I get my inspiration from? Well it started with that 'talkSport' phone call. Ray once said, "follow your heart and your mind will create."

Rough sleeping has always been something close to my heart and something that I am passionate about so when Chelsea Supporters Trust (CST) Chair Cliff Auger and I were speaking shortly after Ray's death at the 'cfcuk' fanzine stall about possible future ideas for the CST to support as part of its community initiatives my heart (and my head told me) we should follow Ray's example and see what we could do to help to homeless by having our own 'Big Sleep Out'.

I cannot say as Chelsea fans that we got there first. I was equally inspired reading about fans from clubs such as Huddersfield Town, Stoke City, Norwich City, Aston Villa and Southampton fans had all blazed a trail raising money for the homeless. Former Manchester United player Lou Macari had set up a 24-bed centre in Stoke to get rough sleepers off the streets of the city.

Everton Under-23 coach David Unsworth launched 'Home Is Where The Heart Is', a campaign to raise money to support people in the City of Liverpool on the brink of homelessness and took his entire academy squad to the 'Goodison Sleep Out'. The campaign was so successful that Unsworth and his Under-23 squad raised £244k, to buy a home for young people at risk of rough sleeping near to Goodison Park.

Soon after, in mid-2018, Cliff and I met with officials at Chelsea and we presented the idea to them about Chelsea hosting its own 'Big Sleep Out'. Then there was another meeting. And another meeting and each meeting we once again explained how simple the idea was: "You just turn up with a sleeping bag and a pillow."

By late 2018, we were sitting waiting knowing that our idea had gone 'upstairs' to the senior echelons of Chelsea Football Club. We waited for the green light and remained patient but watched as more and more clubs began or repeated their own 'Big Sleep Out' events all helping tackle homelessness. We waited a bit more.

Then...

Finally, we got the news we had been waiting for and Saturday, November 16, 2019, was flagged as a free Saturday at Stamford Bridge and the club asked if we wanted to use it for the sleep out. We did not need to be asked twice. Looking at other clubs who had organised sleep outs we set ourselves the target of raising £20,000 and were delighted that we managed to raise £27,000 that would be used by our two chosen charities Glass Door and Oswald Stoll Foundation to make a real difference in many people's lives and get their lives back on track.

So how was it sleeping out at Stamford Bridge with just a piece of cardboard and a sleeping bag for company. It was cold. It was tiring. But, thoroughly worthwhile. At the time Chelsea's marketing gurus were running a campaign 'See it. Hear it. Feel it' in posters around Stamford

Bridge. That night I slept under an advertising board with that catchphrase. 'Feel it? Yes I felt it.'

Being awake on a piece of cardboard on the East Stand concourse at 3am in the morning is probably one of my more unusual Stamford Bridge experiences I have had as a Chelsea supporter. You hear every sound. Including the odd snoring person. You hear the goods train rattling by on the train track behind the East Stand at regular intervals during the night and probably every turn of Tim Rolls book as he is unable to sleep. And you could not fail to hear former Blue Paul Canoville at 4am in the morning wanting to know who John Neal's Assistant Manager was back when he was playing, and no Canners it was not Ernie Whalley! The bacon sandwiches and tea at 6am in the morning laid on by Chelsea FC were most welcome and at the time were probably the best bacon sandwiches and tea I had had for a long time.

The success of the first Big Stamford Bridge Sleep out meant that the conversation with the club about a follow-up in 2020 was a very short conversation. But then Covid 19 happened and our plans to host a follow up had to go into isolation like the rest of the country. But as Chelsea supporters we are anything if not resilient and as the pandemic went from weeks to months and football at Stamford Bridge continued behind closed doors we knew like many other people we had to adapt to doing things virtually so with the Club's support the second 'Big Stamford Bridge Sleep Out' was held virtually as Chelsea fans both here and over land and sea (not sure if anyone was from Leicester) slept in their gardens, their garages, their living rooms, kitchens and the odd shed (but not that Shed) to raise money once more for Oswald Stoll Foundation. The virtual sleep out this time had the support of many former players, Pat Nevin, Nigel Spackman, Paul Canoville, Tommy Langley, Gavin Peacock, Joe Cole and John Sitton who all sent supportive videos and a further £17,000 was raised for a worthwhile cause.

So nearly four years on since Ray's untimely death at just 61 years of age (4 April 2018) on Saturday 26 March 2022 we return to Stamford Bridge for the third 'Big Stamford Bridge Sleep Out', as Chelsea once fans once again get the unique opportunity to sleep out at the home of the World Champions for one night give raise money for our neighbours at Stoll. One night sleeping out at Stamford Bridge cannot recreate what a rough sleeper has to go through every night but we hope those who have taken part before and will take part in future years that it will give them a small insight for one night on what a real rough sleeper has to endure every night.

Thank you, Ray for providing the inspiration for the Stamford Bridge Sleep Out.

If Ray Wilkins with £20 could help a homeless veteran end the cycle of rough sleeping and get his life back on track then we as Chelsea fans want to follow in his footsteps and do the same.

To finish I will go back to where I started and that former homeless veteran who rang into 'talkSport' that day 24-hours after Ray sadly passed away: "Anyone who phones in today with a memory is saying thank you for giving us Ray Wilkins."

Yes. Thank you for giving us Ray Wilkins… and thanks to everybody who has supported the 'Big Stamford Bridge Sleep Out'.

"Follow your heart and your mind will create."

*****

The 'Big Stamford Bridge Sleep Out' is organised by the Chelsea Supporters' Trust with the cooperation of Chelsea Football Club. The event raises funds for Stoll (formerly Sir Oswald Stoll Foundation) whose headquarters are adjacent to Stamford Bridge. Stoll (previously The Sir Oswald Stoll Foundation) provide affordable high-quality housing and support to over 600 people a year. Their work enables vulnerable and disabled Veterans to lead fulfilling and independent lives. Many Veterans have experienced homelessness and Stoll provides advice on housing, financial, wellbeing and huge variety of other issues.

To make an independent donation visit www.stoll.org.uk
Twitter @stoll_veterans

£100 allows a vulnerable Veteran to get support with domestic tasks for a week.
£50 can fund activities to boost mental and physical health for Veterans.
£40 pays for a Health and Wellbeing activity for all Stoll residents.
£10 can provide an hour of essential 1:1 support for a vulnerable veteran.
£5 buys ingredients for one person for a healthy cookery class.

£2 from every copy of 'Tales From The Shed' sold online, and £5 from every copy sold at the 'cfcuk' fanzine stall on Chelsea home match days will be donated to Stoll via the Chelsea Supporters' Trust (CST).

www.chelseasupporterstrust.com
Twitter @ChelseaSTrust

JIM REEVES AND BLUE SUBMARINES
The early days of The Shed
Tim Rolls

Chelsea's match programme, rightly twice winner of the Programme Of The Year award in the mid-1960s, introduced a letters page in 1964, the first to do so. Over the next couple of years, along with complaints about ticket touts and suggestions for club songs, a number of letters were published on the need to improve the atmosphere at Stamford Bridge.

In December 1964 legendary Chelsea supporter Mick Greenaway, now sadly deceased but fondly remembered as a cheerleader by many supporters of that generation, had a letter in the Workington programme, calling for fans at Stamford Bridge to be as vocal as those who travelled away to watch the Blues, especially early in the game. This was the first in a number of programme letters from the ultra-loyal Greenaway on the subject of crowd support and behaviour. He was to make a significant contribution to Chelsea supporter culture over a period of more than a third of a century.

It was exactly at that time, in the early-mid 1960s, that singing and chanting started to become more prevalent at matches. Watching footage of a painful 4-0 defeat at Old Trafford in March 1965, Chelsea chants can clearly be heard and two days later, at the League Cup Final first-leg against Leicester, supporter Barry Holmes remembers it being one of the first times there was singing from under the covered area at the back of the Fulham Road terrace, more crowded than usual despite the low crowd of 20,700 crowd because of heavy rain.

Despite this, atmosphere was not fervent enough for some. That October, in a Daily Mirror article headlined 'Doc Slams the Fans', furious manager Tommy Docherty claimed he was 'sick and disgusted' by the Chelsea supporters. 'They are a waste of time. Useless. I wish we could play all our matches away. A crowd can make a team, can inspire a side. Ours are either silent or critical. There are about 200 who follow us home or away. They are worth their weight in gold. I wouldn't give tuppence for the rest of them'. Among the 200 home and away supporters praised by The Doc were Greenaway and his friends.

Doc's outburst was clearly heartfelt but given the team's poor home form was hardly designed to win friends among many supporters, who duly wrote letters to the national press and the Chelsea programme criticising his stance, pointing out that if the team played better football the crowd would have more to get behind. The Kensington Post responded strongly. 'Perhaps Mr. Docherty should be sick and disgusted at his eleven men rather than the fans. So how about some value for money, then maybe the fans will cheer a little more'.

The atmosphere at Stamford Bridge could be variable but at Fairs Cup games against Roma, Milan and Barcelona that season was excellent and, generally, was improving almost month-by-month. Away, too, support increased in number and in volume. The Newcastle programme that October contained a letter praising Chelsea supporters for their singing and chanting at Fulham and Arsenal, The next away game, at West Bromwich, was on 'Match Of The Day'. Commentator Ken Wolstenholme did a 'to camera' piece at The Hawthorns in front of a bunch of young Chelsea supporters and during the game the strains of "Zigger, Zagger" can clearly be heard. Lifelong supporter Alan Garrison reckons the cheerleader was not Greenaway, who became famous for leading the chant, as the 'Zigger Zagger' was done too quickly. Within a couple of months Docherty was praising the superb vocal support from the 5,000 who travelled to Anfield to watch the famous January 1966 2-1 FA Cup win.

The following month a programme letter urged supporters 'who are prepared to chant and sing throughout the game (to) come and help us at the Fulham Road End'. Many happily did just that. The house-full Leeds FA Cup tie that month was on 'Match Of The Day'. The opening credits show a packed Fulham Road end with, under the covered bit, scarves aloft and banners waved, and the footage shows a delirious surge after Bobby Tambling's winning goal.

Chants of 'Chelsea…Chelsea…Chelsea' can be heard. Supporter Bill Eacott remembers that end singing "Sha-La-La-La Docherty" before matches that season, to the tune of the Small Faces song, and The Doc leaning out of his vantage point above the East Stand and waving back.

In September 1966 Chelsea drew 2-2 with Leicester, 29,800 watching Charlie Cooke and Peter Osgood score before Derek Dougan and Davie Gibson pulled goals back. The Daily Mail thought it was an excellent game and that 'the crowd recognise that Chelsea are slowly settling in to create a framework of fresh teamwork in this much-changed squad'. That game is however remembered by many supporters more for a letter in the programme than anything else.

Fan culture was changing. Singing and chanting was becoming more common, and many clubs had a terraced 'end' where like-minded supporters could really get behind their team. Clifford Webb came up with the name The Shed (apparently derived from Leeds' Scratching Shed South terrace) for the area at the back of the Fulham Road End, the only covered terrace area in the ground. Webb, one of the loyal Chelsea supporters who followed the team home and away and were the 'only real supporters' according to Docherty the previous season, had a letter published announcing that the Fulham Road End, 'where the fanatics stand', would henceforth be called "The Shed". He asked that more people go 'in The Shed and join the singing and chanting, instead of just at big matches like last season's Fairs Cup...If we could have had that support all through the League and cup, we would have won them both. This year we must have this attitude at every game, so please help us make The Shed as fanatical as The Kop'.

Blues supporter for over 50-years David Collis remembers that Webb's letter followed discussions with other die-hard Chelsea supporters including Greenaway, Danny Harkins and Dave Stevens about the need to create a vibrant end at Stamford Bridge.

In those days around 80% of match-going supporters bought a programme so most of the crowd would have noted the name, and the request for like-minded supporters to congregate there. Webb's letter had a definite impact and the name stuck. Increasing numbers of supporters stood, sang and chanted there. The atmosphere at Stamford Bridge significantly improved, though its distance from the pitch, because of the dog track, meant some of the noise was inevitably lost.

Programme Editor Albert Sewell's response was 'Must say "The Shed" sounds a likely place to keep that "Blue Submarine" you've all been singing about. And by the way, don't forget that visiting supporters have a right to shout and sing for their team too'. A rival letter in the programme a few weeks later, from a Peter House of Battersea, suggested The Shed be renamed 'The Foulmouthed End', and argues that the 'fanatics' are a bad advert for the club. Given Peter Houseman came from Battersea and was on occasion the target of unwarranted crowd ire, there must be a possibility this letter was written under an assumed name.

There were a series of letters and articles in match programmes that autumn about obscene chants from The Shed. The press also picked up on this trend. Televised football meant chants would be heard one week and copied all over the country seven days later, and some of the most compelling were indeed slightly rude. One favourite that autumn was a reworking of Jim Reeves' turgid Number One 'Distant Drums', substituting 'Bums' for 'Drums', casting uncomplimentary aspersions about opposing supporters and allowing a mass pointing at them during the 'over there, over there' chorus.

Greenaway had a programme letter printed saying that 'I personally have made persistent attempts to curb the bad language that has been used at various matches, and there is now a crowd of us who will stamp this out with our own methods'. There had been talk in the papers of clubs using plain clothes stewards to address the problem and Greenaway argued, interestingly, that 'there will be no need to persist with the use of Special Branch detectives in plain clothes mixing with the crowd'. He concluded encouragement 'will continue (cleanly) from the chanting, singing, swaying Sheddites'.

Greenaway also had a letter printed in the Daily Express, pointing out that most 'hooligans' were fifteen or sixteen years old and that he and his co-supporters could deal with any unruliness. He also 'wanted to make the Bridge more fanatical than Liverpool's Spion Kop' and referred to Docherty's comment that 'they are the greatest and I wish I had more like them'.

The debate continued. That December the Kensington Post commented on 'a somewhat noisy section behind one goal' (The Shed) at a game, though the Daily Mail made the point that Chelsea 'play home games with away game tactics. No wonder they complain of a lack of atmosphere'. A letter to the programme made the point that there were 'only 400 or so real supporters' and blamed the poor home form on lack of noise, but others flipped the argument, again blaming poor and unattractive team performances for the atmosphere.

The March 1967 crowd of 40,700 at the Sheffield United FA Cup game chanted 'Wembley, here we come' and celebrated raucously. There is a photograph in a later programme showing The Shed at that Sheffield United game waving a host of banners and flags. After that game, following the trend at many other grounds, flags, banners and walking sticks festooned with Chelsea colours were banned from Stamford Bridge after complaints. Clubs across the country were struggling to know how to deal with their more exuberant supporters, Tottenham talking about using vigilantes to curb obscene chanting. The Sun felt that maybe a few black eyes would do the trick.

By the end of that 1966/67 season The Shed was firmly established as the place for young Chelsea supporters to stand, sway, jostle, surge, sing, chant and shout to their heart's content. It was not ideal, being so far from the pitch, but it still had a raucous, boisterous, passionate atmosphere so fondly recalled by Shed denizens over 55 years later. It became home for those who wished to really get behind their team for the next 28 years until it was demolished in 1994, and is warmly remembered by two generations of Chelsea supporters. The name was rightly retained in the rebuilt, all-seater stand and it is to be fervently hoped that it will be kept after any Stamford Bridge redevelopment.

The Shed was named by a supporter, unlike most ends which were named by their club after roads, locations, compass directions or club luminaries. It is an integral part of Chelsea's club history and should always be recognised as such.

This contribution includes extracts from 'Carefree! Chelsea Chants and Terrace Culture' by Mark Worrall and Walter Otton, and also Tim Rolls' book 'Diamonds, Dynamos and Devils: The transformation of Chelsea FC under Tommy Docherty', as well as a piece he wrote for the Club website on The Shed's 50th Anniversary in 2016. Tim has written two further books, 'Stamford Bridge Is Falling Down', and 'Sexton For God', which provide detailed insight into Blues history. You can follow him Twitter @tim_rolls

A JOCK'S LIFE
Cammy McHarg

"To be in love with something that doesn't even know you exist," is one of the more hard-hitting football quotes I've come across in recent times. Mind you, I suspect this would be the case for pretty much any loyal supporter of a football club.

Following your team is a funny old hobby when you think about it – the year-on-year cycle of travelling near and far in order to support them through the good, the bad and the occasionally ugly. The local trips to your home ground, the long journeys for away games, meeting your mates, having a drink and having a moan all before heading home at the end of it all, either high as a kite or absolutely gutted with absolutely no in-between, just to do it all over again the following week. For many of us, it's all we know and we wouldn't have it any other way.

In my 21-years on the planet, my experiences following Chelsea haven't been like those of your typical Stamford Bridge-goer. Being from Glasgow, visits to the place we call home have often been rather infrequent due to the various pesky logistics such as travel, time and finances. Well, at least up until recently.

So, to the question I am asked regularly… "Why Chelsea?" And the answer is very simple really. Most assume it's due to a Chelsea/Rangers ('Blues Brothers') connection or down to the fact that I must have family based in London. The reality is both these theories are incorrect. All of my family live with me in Scotland and I don't have a Scottish team. The reason I am a Chelsea supporter is with huge thanks to my older brother, Robbie.

At just seven-years-old in 1996, Robbie was given a small Ruud Gullit figurine (similar to the ones on sale in the Megastore today) as a late Christmas gift. To the shock of my Dad, Robbie was absolutely over the moon with this – so-much-so that he opted to tune into Chelsea's Fourth Round encounter with Liverpool in the FA Cup the following month. Of course, this just so happened to be the iconic 4-2 victory at Stamford Bridge that came on the road to Chelsea lifting the famous old cup that season, ending a 26-year trophy drought. Robbie followed the entire journey and less shockingly, fell in love instantly and the rest, as they say, is history.

In 1998, my Dad took Robbie to his first ever Chelsea game – the League Cup Final against Middlesbrough where Chelsea triumphed yet again in what was promising to be a very exciting period for supporters. On the day of Robbie's 16th birthday, he undertook a 36-hour round bus trip on his own from Glasgow to London to go and see Chelsea. This became something of a regular feat for him for many years to come. Eventually, his impressive efforts were recognised by the Club when he featured on ITV as part of the 'Sure Fans United' programme.

Due to the fact that Robbie and I have different Mums, as well as a 12-year age gap between us, we have never actually lived together. When I was a young kid, I used to always look forward to spending time with Robbie, when he would often come over to 'see the family'. Looking back, this definitely had nothing to do with the fact that we had all the Sky Sports channels on TV at my home and must have been by some mad coincidence that his visits almost always seemed to coincide with each Chelsea game that he wasn't down in London for! So, despite growing up in an environment surrounded by friends and family who ninety-nine times out of a hundred, supported either Rangers or Celtic, I ultimately had no choice in the end... did I?

Throughout my early teens, the opportunities to attend Chelsea games in the flesh were often few and far between. This was due to the supervision responsibilities, the absences required from school and/or work and, of course, the cost of travel, accommodation and match tickets. When all of this was taken into account, it tended to be quite a tricky hobby to work around. Fortunately, despite not being a Chelsea fan himself, my Dad was always very accommodating and supportive of my passion and used to take me to the Bridge at least twice a season, generally as Birthday and Christmas presents.

When I turned 17, my folks remained reluctant to let me travel to London on my own. They saw it as being 'too dangerous' for someone my age. One day, I grew unwilling to oblige with these rules for any longer and went ahead and booked tickets and travel for a Chelsea vs. West Brom game one Monday night. Let's just say my Mum was less than impressed when I unveiled these plans the night before my departure.

After a relatively successful trip, I made it my goal to make it down for at least one game a month from this point onwards. Sometimes I would be accompanied by Robbie, but more-often-than-not it was just me, myself and I. At this point in time, I knew very few London-based Chelsea supporters, so these trips tended to be extremely long, anti-social and just plain boring whilst travelling. For each game I attended, it usually worked out as a more-or-less exactly 24-hour round trip from Glasgow, by the time I leave my home one day and return the following. That said, to this day each trip remains just as worth it as the next one.

On to more recent times and Frank Lampard's stint as manager was by far the most 'attached' I have ever felt to Chelsea Football Club. My undisputed boyhood hero taking charge of a Blues squad with a core of five or six academy products was something I had never experienced in my lifetime but something I had always dreamed of as a kid.

In the first half of the 2019/20 season, Robbie and I followed Chelsea everywhere on a regular basis. Having booked up a trip to Munich for the Champions League Round of 16 affair against Bayern, whilst enjoying an unexpected push for a top four finish and with what promised to be a very busy transfer window just around the corner, things couldn't have been more exciting for me as a Chelsea fan at that point in time. Of course, the excitement was to be short-lived as the world was put on hold after the COVID-19 pandemic struck. At this point, the footballing dynamic would dramatically change right across the globe for the following 18-months or so. Notably, the absence of supporters in football grounds was a huge eye-opener for me and became a catalyst in my relentless attendance in the 2021/22 campaign.

During this period, I missed the rest of Frank Lampard's career as Chelsea boss before his unfortunate dismissal in January 2021 - a decision that absolutely devastated me at the time. A few months down the line came the small matter of the European Cup triumph in Porto in May 2021 (a trip that Robbie and I narrowly missed out on, after booking flights and hotels only for the COVID-19 travel criteria to intervene). Sandwiched in between the contrasting emotions of these events came the European Super League fiasco where for a period, it seemed we were going to lose everything we loved about Chelsea.

A combination of these factors provided me with a valuable 'kick up the back side' - I came to the realisation that following Chelsea near and far (even all the way from Scotland) is exactly how I want to live my life. The club is everything I have ever known and I no longer want to miss out on these precious memories. I refused to let the distance be a barrier any longer. Much of this decision was inspired by fellow Chelsea supporter and cult hero, Terry Komatsu, who travelled over from Japan by himself to become a Chelsea Season Ticket Holder.

In order to make this work, I had to make some big changes in my life - I found a new, better paid Monday-Friday job in order to ensure I am able to fund weekly visits down South and to get my weekends back. I also had to make sacrifices in my personal/social life too, reducing the time I spent with my local mates as well as putting my plans to move out and buy a flat on hold.

Thanks to the power of social media, I have met countless like-minded Chelsea supporters such as Terry who are able to share their amazing tales whilst following the Club down the years with me, every single weekend. Many of these once-strangers have rapidly become close friends in recent times and in doing so, have totally changed the dynamic behind my visits to Stamford Bridge Nowadays, my trips are more enjoyable than they ever have been.

Moving forward, the long-term plan for myself and Robbie is to become Stamford Bridge Season Ticket Holders. We appreciate just how spoiled with success we have been in our lifetimes and we appreciate that this hasn't always been the case for Chelsea fans. And maybe someday, the less-than-glorious times will return, and if that happens I shall still be there. I want to eventually be the one who's passing on tales of following this great Club. Long may my Chelsea story continue!

You can keep up with Cammy's adventures watching Chelsea over Hadrian's Wall, land and sea on Twitter @carefreecammy

AZUL ES EL COLOR!
'Spanish' Ken Turner

I was born on May 2, 1940, in Dawes Road, some three-quarters of a mile from Stamford Bridge. My father Fred Turner, the second eldest of eleven children, hailed from Britannia Road, opposite the ground! The Turner's were 'Blue' through and through. My Uncle Henry was described by David Miller, former Chief Sports Correspondent of the 'Daily Express' and 'The Times', and to whom he dedicated his book 'Cup Magic', as a man whose "passion for the game of almost fifty years has been spent unremittingly hooked on glorious uncertainty, that even the vagaries of Chelsea have failed to diminish his ardour;" a sentiment most true blue fans will identify with I'm sure.

My earliest memories were of the sound of bombs and ack-ack gunfire as nightly raids by German aircraft attempted to deprive me of a future lifetime of highs and lows as a Chelsea supporter. By the age of six, however, the most memorable sound to be heard in the basement flat at 44 Dawes Road was the roar on a Saturday afternoon when Chelsea scored! Saturday afternoons were not the best time for a siesta in our house! At that time, my Dad was Assistant General Manager of the now-defunct Regent Palace Hotel, just off Piccadilly Circus. In those days, it was the largest hotel in Europe, capable of sleeping 1700 guests a night. On August 30, 1947, Dad had a day off and decided I was old enough to attend my first match at 'The Bridge'. It was the third game of the 1947/48 season and Chelsea beat Derby County 1-0 with a first-half goal scored by legendary striker Tommy Lawton. It was nice to get off to a winning start! It may be over 70 years ago, but I've never forgotten the thrill of being passed over the heads of others down to the front. From the age of ten, I went to the games on my own and in those days we had crowds of 60 to 70,000 so, as you can imagine, at the final whistle there was quite a crush to experience when leaving the ground. I recall often leaving by the 'Bovril' steps and my feet never touching the ground until I was out on the Fulham Road! Needless to say, 'Health & Safety' was yet to be 'invented'!

One of the 'must have' things back then was a rattle. Dad got me a super-dooper one, it had Southern Railways engraved in black on one side and its original purpose was to warn track workers of oncoming trains... just the thing to ensure my support was heard in a crowd of 65,000! My short journey to 'The Bridge' took me past the Granville Theatre of Varieties, opposite Green & London the ironmongers. In those days the Granville was famous for its staging of nude performances. Of course the 'artistes' were not allowed to move and so they performed as statues... not that I was ever permitted to view a live performance. Outside however, they displayed an array of photographs which for an 11-year-old was quite informative and, indeed, revealing... even though the whole truth was hidden if you get my meaning!

The thing I've always loved about our Chelsea is the great character we have shown consistently in adversity, and nowhere was this more evident than in the 1950/51 season when, bottom of the league, we needed to win our last four games, which we duly did, however we also required the results of fellow strugglers Everton and Sheffield Wednesday to go our way. Our final match was against Bolton Wanderers and Chelsea needed to win by more than three goals, we won 4-0 and avoided relegation by 0.044 of a goal... you couldn't make it up!

As it happened, games back then were quite often were the stuff of fantasy and I remember a couple of 11-goal thrillers at the Bridge... yes, 11 goals in a single match!

1) Chelsea played Manchester United in the early part of their maiden First Division title-winning season of 1954/55. October 16, 1954,... we lost 5-6! Imagine if you had not been at the game and you were listening to the scores via Charles Buchan's 'Sports Report' on the wireless in your motor car and the announcer read, "Chelsea five, Manchester United.....six!!!" You'd probably have jammed the brakes on and caused a crash! But what a match it was. Seamus O'Connell, an amateur from Ireland, was handed a debut by our manager Ted Drake and scored a hat-trick and Dennis Viollet mirrored O'Connell's feat for United! Only one other player has scored a hat-trick on their debut for Chelsea. September 1, 1906, (well before my time!), George 'Gatling Gun' Hilsdon rattled home five goals in a 9-2 win over Glossop! As well as O'Connell, Chelsea fielded another amateur in that game against Man U... Jim Lewis, a centre-forward signed from Walthamstow Avenue who were one of the most successful non-league sides of the 1950s.

2) I vividly recall when we played Newcastle United (September 10, 1958) and this time we won an absolute cracker 6-5. Just four months older than me at that time, the teenage 'goal machine' that was Jimmy Greaves scored twice. What a privilege it was to have watched him from the start of his career and what wouldn't we give to have him at the peak of his powers in the Chelsea squad today? Football has never seen a finisher like him. Of course, in those days, there was no supporter segregation, and why would there be when we were all there to enjoy a football match? Indeed, part of the enjoyment was the banter to be had between rival fans. Standing that day on the terraced end that would later be christened The Shed with a bunch of Geordies, whose pleasure from a trip to London, one imagines, was yet to properly begin, was one

of my outstanding footballing memories.

Probably my happiest Chelsea recollections were the two FA Cup Final matches against 'Dirty' Leeds United for our first ever triumph in the competition in 1970. The Wembley game was a huge disappointment. The hallowed turf that every player dreamt of playing on in front of the iconic twin towers resembled a cabbage patch! It has been widely written that the 'Horse of the Year Show' had been staged two weeks previously and this ruined the surface. True or not, the pitch was ill-prepared for a game of football and had been sanded so much by the groundsmen that the ball didn't bounce consistently. At times it was a farce.

I had tickets for the match but found myself in Rome on company business! Fortunately, the match was shown on Eurovision, so I was able to watch it on a big screen in the ballroom of the Hotel Quirinale... support from afar is equally important! What character we showed in coming from behind twice to force the first ever FA Cup Final replay against a team that was, arguably, the best in the league at that time; the attitude Chelsea showed was a fine example of what makes us supporters love our team, and so it was on to Old Trafford!

That magnificent night in Manchester, spent with my dear old dad who, year-after-year, put a bet on Chelsea to win the Cup, except that year! What matches they were, these finals. Crunching tackles that would not be allowed today were met with players jumping up shrugging their shoulders and getting on with the game... no rolling around and feigning injury or trying to con the ref. No groups of players surrounding the referee menacingly and disputing his decisions. Here is another interesting fact, none of the players in this or any other match I had watched hitherto found it necessary to roam the pitch spitting profusely at every conceivable opportunity. The speed of these games was fantastic, and I would urge anyone who hasn't watched them in full to do so; it's terrific stuff and Ossie's equaliser at Old Trafford is my favourite ever Chelsea goal. Shown from behind the goal, Ossie dummies their keeper, David Harvey, with his header! Into extra-time again and David Webb's header delivered the goods... at last we had won the FA Cup. It's fair to say that Don Revie's team was not a popular one and this was exemplified when they left the ground without collecting their losers medals!

How lucky I was to have been around when the likes of my hero, the 'King', Peter Osgood, strutted his stuff alongside Alan Hudson, Ian Hutchinson, Charlie Cooke, Peter Houseman, John Hollins, Eddie McCreadie, Ron Harris, Peter Bonetti, among others, all of whom came from within our British shoreline and entertained us on pitches which saw no grass, only mud and sand from October to early April. Young people watching videos of the games my heroes played in can be forgiven for believing that the 'forever' green surfaces played on today were ever thus.

TALES FROM THE SHED

In the modern era, my devotion for Chelsea has been expressed from afar as I retired to live in Spain many moons ago. I do however still return to my beloved Stamford Bridge to catch a game or two when visiting family 'back home'. Adios for now my friends, and as we say here, where I am able to watch every Blues match on my illegal I.P.T.V. system for €10 a month, 'Azul es el color!'

'Spanish' Ken isn't on social media but he loves chatting Chelsea via email. You can write to Ken via kenandfinna@gmail.com

WHY I CHOSE THE SHED
Rowanne Westhenry

Although my blood is blue it's via transplant rather than inherited. I got into football when it nearly came home in 1996 and was able to blag it in the playground for a little while until I had to pick a club to support. At the time, the choice was between Arsenal or Manchester United, and as I was from London it seemed like a no brainer. I went home and told my Tottenham Hotspur-loving Dad that I was going to support Arsenal like my mates at school. "That's nice," he said. "Where are you going to live?" He sat me down to watch 'Match of the Day' on Sunday morning and I fell in love with a team that had the best player I had ever seen in the form of Gianfranco Zola. People took the p*ss because we'd last won the league in black and white, but they quickly quietened down when we won the FA Cup that season.

Because of my mixed heritage (My Mum's father was in the army but hailed from Salford so she's Man U) it wasn't until 2002 that I made my first trip to Stamford Bridge. I sat in the Matthew Harding Lower and watched through the net on the goal as we beat Preston North End 3-1 in the Fifth Round of the FA Cup. Chelsea drew Spurs away in the next round and Dad took me to Three Point Lane where I had to stay quiet while we beat them 4-0. I inadvertently let out a chuckle when the fourth went in and even though I was a 14-year-old girl, we had to shuffle off The Shelf pretty sharpish.

In the following years I managed to make it to at least a couple of games a season, mostly FA Cup matches, and would usually sit in the Matthew Harding Lower. When I got a job that paid well in 2008 I made it my mission to get a season ticket, mainly so that I wouldn't have to miss out again like I had with Moscow. The only home games I missed in the 2008/09 season were while I was working abroad in Spain for a month, and I sat in every stand to test them out.

I was in the East Lower for the 4-0 win over Bordeaux in the Champions League and it felt weird to be sat so close to people who were singing and showing support but surrounded by silence in that stand. True, I could see the Bordeaux players jogging in ridiculous puffa jackets, and got to serenade Frank Lampard as he warmed up, but the lack of atmosphere made me check that stand off my list pretty quickly. The upper tier was ticked off too when I watched a 1-1 draw with Manchester United, just four months after the heartbreak in Moscow. It's too steep both in gradient and price to be offering that little in the way of atmosphere. Honestly, even the away section at Ajax felt safer than sitting up there did.

The West Stand wasn't much better, although the view from the lower tier is among the best in the ground. When my work stint in Spain finished I got on the plane, handed off my suitcase at Heathrow and jumped straight on the tube to watch us lose 2-1 against Arsenal. I sat about seven rows back and right on the halfway line I could see everything and it would have been perfect if anyone else fancied singing. Sitting in the upper tier for the 4-4 draw with Liverpool in the Champions League and the atmosphere was a bit livelier, especially when the Scousers who'd bought home tickets outed themselves when they went 1-0 up and had to be removed by the stewards, but I could tell it wasn't like that all the time. Padded seats and heaters though, it's proper posh up there!

I went back to the Matthew Harding Lower for one game, and it was *that* Barcelona game (May 6, 2009). Sat underneath the clock I went absolutely mental when Michael Essien's screamer hit the net at the other end. When Gerard Pique committed the most blatant handball ever seen, it was right in my eyeline. When Victor Valdes picked up the ball I was convinced he was going to place it on the spot for the penalty we were definitely going to get given. When he hoofed it up the pitch I lost all sense of reason. I had to make a choice after that whether I was going to get home safely or get myself a lengthy stadium ban. I made it back to my local pub in time to neck enough shots to kill my feelings. The Matthew Harding Stand was tarnished from then on.

All of that left The Shed. I'd sat there for the opening game of the season when we demolished Portsmouth 4-0, in January 2009 when we beat Stoke City in the last minute of the game, and when we spent the whole of the last home game of the campaign against Blackburn Rovers singing that we wanted Guus Hiddink to stay. I loved being so close to the away fans and being able to respond to them, I loved being so close to the pitch, and I especially loved the history of the stand. The fact that it's the easiest to get into and out of, and the cheapest alongside the Matthew Harding Lower, was just the icing on the cake.

Even though I'd been to every home game bar two and spent over £1500 on tickets over the season, I didn't qualify for a ticket for the FA Cup Final that year. That only made me more determined to get my season ticket sorted. I had plenty of points so I put down The Shed Lower as my first choice on the application form and took it to the box office in person on my way to work. To this day I'm convinced that that's why I got assigned a seat in row one, right on the edge of the 18-yard box. That's where I sat when we won the Premier League the following season and Didier Drogba blanked me during the celebrations because I'd shouted at him to get up off the floor early in the game. I was there when Oscar scored a worldie against Juventus and I missed it because I was arguing with a steward about the UEFA man with a stick blocking my view. I was there when Theo Walcott, playing for Arsenal at the time, chased a futile ball and I laughed right in his face, which he seemed to find funny himself.

There are downsides to sitting pitchside of course. My view of the game is restricted to the final third, and my depth perception is so messed up that I start screaming "SHOOT!" as soon as the ball crosses the halfway line. Sometimes players take my tactical advice to "go to him" to heart and concede needless fouls, and I've ended up in a number of unflattering press photos of the crowd. I have a steward sat in front of me for the last 10 minutes of every game, and I get displaced for the away fans for all the FA Cup games and some later stage Champions League ones. Despite all that, I wouldn't swap my seat for anything.

Like most people, COVID forced me to re-evaluate my relationship with football. Having no option but to watch games on television with no fans in the stadium made me realise just how important being there is to my love of the game. I don't mind watching one or two games a season from the comfort of my own sofa, but football isn't a spectacle to enjoy at a distance. It's an opportunity to be part of something bigger, to sing the songs sung by generations before you and those to come, to give your energy to the players when they're running on fumes. The sense of community is akin to a religion, only our Gods are mortal and, in my case, can hear my prayers. It also emphasised how important we as fans are to the game, bringing an atmosphere to what is otherwise just 22 men kicking a ball around. It doesn't matter as much without us.

When it was announced that we could go back for the start of the 2021-22 season it was a nerve-wracking time. Although my direct seat neighbours and I have a group chat where we had been checking in on each other, we didn't know how many of our fellow fans wouldn't be coming back. Thankfully we all made it through and seeing everyone together again just confirmed what I had known for the past 12 years: The Shed is my home!

Rowanne is @agirlintheshed on Twitter as well as in real life. Based in West London, she's either on the wrong side of a bar or writing words for money.

THE NIGHT THE LIGHTS WENT OUT
Vince Cooper

In January 1969 I was 12-years-old and halfway through my first year at secondary school. I had been going to Stamford Bridge regularly with my Dad, Brother, Uncles, Cousins and various friends. We always stood in the same place (just to the right of The Shed as you look down at the pitch - up the stairs, turn right) and I regularly went to Football Combination and Youth Team matches on the weekends when the first team were playing away.

The Blues had built a good team, regularly competing near the top of the First Division and reaching the later stages of the FA Cup along with some good performances in Europe, but almost as regularly falling just short (the 1965 League Cup success was the only time we 'got over the line' and, to be honest, the competition wasn't held in great esteem back then). But Chelsea played exciting football. Peter Osgood was, of course, the hero of the Bridge - and around him, first Tommy Docherty and then Dave Sexton had put together plenty of great supporting players. From Peter Bonetti in goal to the likes of Bobby Tambling, Charlie Cooke, David Webb, John Hollins and many more, there was plenty of talent worth going to the Bridge to watch.

In November 1968 an injury to Hollins saw Sexton try Ossie out in an unfamiliar right-half position with Alan Birchenall leading the attack. The experiment had mixed results and was certainly unpopular with the majority of fans but the manager persisted and when Hollins returned to the line-up it was in the problem position of right-back.

The Blues had already been knocked out of two competitions with Derby County overcoming our boys in a League Cup Third Round replay and DWS Amsterdam winning a coin toss to end Fairs Cup interest. With a nine-point gap to Liverpool at the top of the First Division table, January rolled around with the FA Cup the only real hope left of a successful season.

Second Division Carlisle United were dispatched 2-0 at Stamford Bridge in the Third Round thanks to first-half goals from Osgood and Tambling and the Blues were rewarded with a Fourth Round trip to play another second-tier team, Preston North End.

We watched 'World of Sport' and read in the following day's newspapers that Chelsea had outclassed their rivals but failed to find the net, a goalless draw bringing the Lancashire team to London four days later for the replay.

Whilst the front pages of Tuesday's newspapers had stories about a dustman's strike in South London, Richard Nixon's first day in office as the U.S. President and the cost of a loaf of bread going up by 1d to 1/8 this 12-year-old football - and Chelsea - fanatic immediately turned to the back pages and I was happy to read the news that Osgood would play, despite suffering a thigh injury in the first encounter.

So, on a soaking wet evening we made our way through Battersea Park and over the Thames to form part of the 44,000 plus crowd. It was plain-sailing. Ian Hutchinson, signed the previous summer from Cambridge United, scored his first goal for the club to set the Blues on their way in the first-half and Birchenall doubled the lead not long after half-time.

Chelsea were coasting and we were already looking forward to a Fifth Round tie with Stoke City ten days later. Then disaster struck, although not in the way anyone might have expected. With 20-minutes to go half of the floodlights went out (apparently caused by a fire in the control system). The referee continued and we peered through the murk as our team made their way to the last 16. Suddenly, more lighting disappeared and one side of the pitch was in almost total darkness. The players were brought off as staff tried to fix the problem but they failed and the match was eventually abandoned. With no guarantee that the floodlights would be fit for action in time and the 5th Round looming, it was decided that the match would be replayed on Monday afternoon at 3pm.

In the meantime, the Blues travelled to Southampton and, with Osgood, Cooke and John Boyle on the sidelines and Alan Hudson making his debut along with new signing John Dempsey they were thrashed 5-0.

So, a Monday afternoon kick-off with everyone back to work or school, meagre attendance surely? Well…

My school, Battersea County, was probably made up of 75% Blues fans and as soon as it was announced that the rearranged match would be an afternoon kick-off, plans were hatched. As a First Year at the school, the idea of 'bunking off' had never crossed my mind. Older kids did it, I was aware of it, but actually doing it myself hadn't yet crossed my mind. An enquiry about the possibility of 'going sick' was quickly dismissed by my mum so, if I wanted to go, I would have to take the plunge. I weighed it up. I heard of so many who were going that I decided that if I was going to get into trouble for it, I certainly wouldn't be on my own. It could be the biggest detention ever!

It was also my first match 'alone' - without the family and friends who were my regular co-attendees. So, even though I was in my school uniform it also felt, somehow so 'grown-up'.

So, after going out for lunch we just… never went back. A group of us made our way to the ground arriving a good hour before kick-off to find - thousands there in various school uniforms. Battersea County clearly wasn't the only school to suffer low attendance on that Monday afternoon.

And those of us there (the attendance was an official 36,522 which considering many of us would duck under the gate might have been considerably higher) saw some real drama.

My schoolmate and I stood further over than my usual family position, down below the mighty Shed, populated by 'bigger boys'. We cheered as the team ran out with Ossie, Cooke and Boyle all back in the line-up but Preston shocked everyone when they took an early lead through Gerry Ingram. Still, there was plenty of time to come back. But as the match went on the visitors, with future star Archie Gemmill seemingly everywhere (think a Scottish, N'Golo Kante) were holding on.

Half-time came and went; anxiety levels grew, we tried to help the team by singing louder but it didn't seem to help. It turned into a siege on the visiting goal. Ossie was pushed up front, we attacked almost non-stop. Then Preston broke and Gemmill popped up to smash a shot against the bar. We breathed a collective sigh of relief and sang out (probably in a slightly higher pitch than the crowd might usually have sounded with the high schoolboy element present): "Score, score, when we get one we'll get more..."

Finally, in the very last minute, a hero arrived. David Webb, occasional goalkeeper, popped up in the Preston area and headed home (something he was to do even more famously at Old Trafford a year later). It might have been from a Charlie Cooke cross but my memory isn't 'that' good.

Injury-time. No boards from fourth officials, no Tannoy announcements so nobody knew how long was left. Long enough though, for Cooke to smash the winner through a crowded penalty area. Cue delirium. All worries about about impending school punishments (or any handed out by my mum if word got back to her) were forgotten as we celebrated as though we'd won the cup.

I don't think any 'punishment' was actually handed out at school and my mum thankfully never found out. I remember our headmaster, Mr Deadman, mentioning it in severe terms at assembly and promising retribution if it occurred again but that was it, we were in the clear. The decision had clearly been reached that it would be impossible to punish what seemed like half the school!

Five days later I was back at the Bridge, back with the family/friends group to see another thriller as we saw off Stoke City 3-2, Ossie scoring twice and Alan Birchenall getting the other, to keep the Wembley dream alive.

Sadly that dream died at the quarter-final stage when holders West Brom came to Stamford Bridge and recorded a 2-1 win. So we had to wait for our cup hopes to be fulfilled, although only for one more year before finally achieving the goal on a memorable night at Old Trafford - another amazing occasion to reminisce about. Chelsea have given me so many but that win over Preston - coincidentally the opposition for my first-ever visit to Stamford Bridge as a six-year-old back in 1963 - will always live in my memory.

Vince Cooper is the author of 'Blue Army: The 25 Men Who Made Chelsea' and manages 'The League' website which features many fantastic articles and photographs about football history. You can follow Vince on Twitter @Theleaguemag

GLORY-HUNTER
Kraig Dixon

I still remember the first time I was called a 'glory-hunter'; it was 1998 and the start of a new school year, Chelsea had just beaten Real Madrid to add the UEFA Super Cup to the Cup Winners' Cup all thanks to the FA Cup triumph over Middlesbrough at Wembley the year before that. My celebrations clearly put noses out of joint and a new kid dropped the G-bomb. I was stunned – this was a term I'd used myself for years in Home Counties playgrounds, towards friends who professed their support for Liverpool and Manchester United. And here I was, for the first time, on the other side of that insult.

There were fellow pupils there who'd known me all my life who soon put the accuser straight about my long-time allegiance to the Blues, but I wasn't bothered by what I'd just been labelled. Alongside the amusement and enjoyment of it all, for the first time it actually felt like Chelsea had made it. It was funny to think that other football fans considered someone would support the Club just because we were successful!

I was still only 14-years-old when this happened, so compared to a lot of supporters at the time, I was lucky; the last time they'd have been able to celebrate a Chelsea side who'd won the FA Cup and European trophy was at the very beginning of the 1970s. Of course, there were enjoyable promotion campaigns in the meantime but if you're talking about major honours, fans of a certain vintage would have been waiting the best part of 26-years to see their side lift major silverware.

I wasn't there in 1997 to see that wait come to end, however I had already been present at Wembley to see Chelsea win a trophy. I can't remember the exact month or year when I became a Chelsea fan but on March 25, 1990, I went to my first match, which would be the first of around 700 and counting. My Dad took me on the short journey to the home of football to see the Blues under the famous old twin towers, where we took on Middlesbrough - it was ALWAYS Middlesbrough - in the Zenith Data Systems Cup Final. For those who don't know what the ZDS Cup is, it was the Full Members' Cup rebranded for sponsorship purposes. Still confused? Between 1985 and 1992, before the Premier League was founded, teams from the top two flights were invited to play in what was essentially a fourth domestic competition. It wasn't a cherished honour by any means; however, the record books show that nobody won it more than Chelsea who had beaten Manchester City 5-4 in front of a packed Wembley in its inaugural season.

Our second triumph came against 'Boro, in what would be the first of three Wembley Cup wins over the Teessiders in the space of eight years, with a Tony Dorigo free-kick sealing victory. I still have the programme, a scarf that my Dad bought me along Wembley Way and a fully intact match ticket, as I recall the old boy operating the turnstiles letting me go through without tearing off the side of it. Not every football supporter's lucky enough to say their first match ended with their team winning silverware, especially at the most famous stadium in world football. And despite the ZDS Cup's humble status, to me as a six-year-old, seeing Dave Beasant lifting that huge, glistening trophy was incredible. However, I knew even then that wasn't what football was like for the majority of the time and although I enjoyed that day as if we'd been crowned World Champions, I was fully aware that Chelsea winning major trophies had at that point been unique generational events. I didn't care, I loved it and over the next few years, I watched my team from every side & corner of the Bridge with just a couple of cup runs to really cling onto in that time, including a devastating albeit unlucky hammering in 1994's FA Cup Final.

To then see the class of '97 replicate what the mythical 1970 team had done and actually win the FA Cup again felt like that was 'it'. We'd been on the rise for a couple of years or so leading up to that, and winning major honours whilst playing mostly great football, finally made people on the outside look at Chelsea the same way I'd felt about them throughout my childhood. Despite the disappointment of getting so close to the Premier League title but ultimately falling short in 1998/99, I was happy enough just knowing that I'd seen us win major honours with some fantastic players and it wasn't unthinkable to do so again. Indeed, we won another trophy the following season and we even went close to overcoming the mighty Barcelona at the Camp Nou to reach the final four in our first ever Champions League campaign, an incredible journey which has possibly been overshadowed and underrated in the years since.

Depending on who you listen to, Roman Abramovich's purchase of the club in 2003 either accelerated the rise of a club on the up or prevented a repeat of what happened after our last spell of success when Chelsea almost went out of business and the team nearly wound up in the third-tier of English football for the first time in its history. Who knows what would have happened if the Russian's plane hadn't soared over SW6 on his way to become a football club owner - we've had a lot of 'what-if' moments, from being persuaded not to enter the inaugural European Cup in 1955 to the fall-out over Eddie McCreadie's car and his subsequent departure, and plenty more besides. For what at the time was a rare occasion, things fell in our favour that fateful day. When some rivals sing that we have 'no history', I often chuckle and implore them to spend some time looking through a club biography.

We know of course that what they mean is, that Chelsea didn't always win stuff. Through the prism of a glory-hunter, who chooses to support a team they know is likely to win things, the two can become conflated. But it doesn't matter anymore because, under Roman's rule, success was no longer just something to be enjoyed for a couple of years or so, then denied for decades; it was clear from day one that this was a new, improved Chelsea and sure enough, for the first time in 50-years and only the second time in 100, we were crowned League champions. Depending on your age, 1970 or 1997 was thought to be the pinnacle of supporting Chelsea but being there in Bolton to watch Frank Lampard put the seal on the title win in 2005 felt like nothing before. It felt just as good hammering our nearest challengers Manchester United a year later to confirm back-to-back Premier Leagues. The three Premier League title-winning seasons since then weren't too bad either! Not to mention numerous further cup triumphs and records broken along the way making us the most successful team in England since the Abramovich takeover, and there's no sign of the silverware stopping. We all came to support the Club at different times and in different ways, but I'm sure we can all pretty much agree that there's nothing quite as good as 'making history, not reliving it'.

Now that we have won it all - and all over again - we're spoilt for choice in picking our greatest ever Chelsea memory. I've already listed a few that'll probably be in the top five of many a list and we're fortunate that there are numerous other candidates which I've not even had the time to mention. Arguably our most important have been the 1983 victory over Bolton to retain second-tier status and 2003's victory over Liverpool to ensure Champions League football ahead of Mr. Abramovich's arrival however, given all the pain and misfortune that we suffered over the seasons leading up to it and the frankly unbelievable way we finally achieved it, 2012's Champions League victory will probably be the number one for most, perhaps with the 2021 victory in the same competition giving it a run for it its money. I was lucky to be there for both triumphs and I must admit that being the Champions of Europe is a feeling that trumps them all. And Munich probably just pips Porto, albeit choosing between the two is a bit like being asked who your favourite child is.

However, despite so many candidates, my favourite match of all time has to be the Champions League semi-final 2012 against Barcelona. Back at the scene of our first CL exit, in the years between quite a rivalry had built up thanks to Mourinho, Frisk, Øvrebø and all that. Whilst things were still fairly even in terms of head-to-heads between the two in that time, and there were spells when I think we could have legitimately claimed to be the best team in Europe, out of the two only the Catalans had actually gone on to win the famous big-eared trophy and by the time of this meeting were being lauded by some as the greatest club side of all time. Whereas Chelsea were, on paper at least, arguably in our worst shape of the Abramovich-era, with managerial chaos, patchy Premier League form and a squad with many players who could have been forgiven for wondering whether this trophy would elude them given what had gone before.

Even going to Barcelona with a 1-0 first leg didn't fill me with any real confidence that we could win the tie and reach a second Champions League final in our history. There were still some great players in our squad of course and the comeback win over Napoli in an earlier round showed the mentality that had by now become synonymous with Chelsea was still very much there, but I just didn't fancy us as a team good enough to be challenging to win a competition of this prestige anymore. In some respects that took the pressure off, and I just wanted to enjoy being there for an occasion like this, without expectations, unlike some of my previous trips there which were very intense. That said, walking to the ground, there was proof of that aforementioned rivalry all along the way with dog's abuse and even beer cans being fired in our direction from home fans outside bars lining the route!

Having got through that unscathed and enthused by it all, I went to enter the stadium only to realise that my wallet – containing about 100 Euros, my bank cards but most importantly, my match ticket, was not in my pocket! After double-checking multiple times, I realised I'd fallen foul of one of the notorious local pickpockets so went to the ticket office at the stadium but unsurprisingly they didn't want to know. Some of my mates were starting to go in and I was starting to panic when suddenly, a tout appeared almost out of nowhere waving an away ticket in my face, demanding hundreds of Euros for it. To this day I have no idea what happened to my original ticket but with adrenaline and a few hours' worth of Estrella flowing through me, I was absolutely convinced the one he was provocatively dangling in front of my nose was mine that he'd pinched off me, so in what seemed like a split second, I snatched it off him and marched towards the rest of my pals at the turnstiles who couldn't believe what they were witnessing! I won't repeat what I said to the tout as he initially tried following me once he got over the shock of what I'd done but regardless of my 5ft 8in, 160-pound frame, my words and the manner of which I said them was enough to stop him from even attempting to get it back off me - nothing was going to stop me from being there to see this game and thankfully, given what unfolded, nothing did!

Throughout the game itself, with all our injuries, the John Terry red card, going two goals down in the first half and conceding a penalty in the second, I was convinced we were going to get hit by a 2009 style sucker punch which would hurt in the morning even more than the lost wallet, and even just before the ball broke for Fernando Torres to score the goal that meant we knew we were going to Munich, my mate and I were talking about how well we'd done to take them as far as we did before the seemingly inevitable Barca winning goal which thankfully never came. And the rest, as they say, is history!

We ended up celebrating throughout the night, and a couple of us sharing a room fell asleep. With dead phone batteries and no alarm to wake us up, we missed our flight back to Luton and so had to fork out for later flights to Gatwick Airport. Fortunately my mate covered my costs as well as I had no way of paying myself. From Gatwick we traipsed to Luton to pick up the car and drove home from there. And do you know what, neither of us cared one bit! Just like being labelled a glory-hunter for the first time, the joy of Chelsea winning meant that I was simply carefree!

Kraig Dixon is a Matthew Harding Lower season ticket holder, Chelsea Pitch Owner, Chelsea Supporters Trust member and 'cfcuk' fanzine scribe, you can follow him on Twitter @BecauseWeMust05

THE SHEPHERD'S BUSH MALDINI
Kelvin Barker

You know those ones where you spend too much time over-thinking a situation, when you know all along what you're going to do: That shirt costs £100 and you've only got eighty quid in the bank, so should you buy it? Well, you'll look a million dollars wearing it, so it's your moral duty to make the purchase really. The wider public will thank you. Or the missus has got the right hump and is getting on your wick, but are you going to say something? No chance, it's not worth the aggro. And to be honest, you're a bit frightened of her when she's got the hump. Or Roger Freestone's just dropped one in the net and Chelsea have lost again, but will you be back for more punishment next week? Of course you will. Life wasn't supposed to be easy.

Well, Sheffield Wednesday away was one of those.

I started permanent work with a Civil Service job in a Shepherds Bush office block on 20th August 1984 (five days before the famous 'Chelsea Here, Chelsea There' game at Highbury, which marked the Blues' return to English football's top-flight after five years away. Because there's *always* a Chelsea connection to every date). The following month, on the afternoon of September 26 (Chelsea v Millwall, League Cup Second Round, first leg. Won 3-1. Carnage), a trial took place on an Astroturf pitch in Kennington to select the regional football team to take part in that season's national Civil Service cup competition. In my 19-year-old desperation to impress all my new colleagues, I embarrassed myself with a performance so bad that I missed out entirely on selection, despite the standard really being pretty average. I was mortified.

The first round of the tournament kicked off for my region's team on the afternoon of November 14 (Turkey 0 England 8. With first and second choice strikers Mark Hateley and Paul Mariner unavailable, it seemed certain that the prolific Kerry Dixon would get his long-awaited first call up to the national team. Instead, manager Bobby Robson typically opted for Aston Villa's trusty but unexceptional number nine, Peter Withe, who failed to find the target despite the one-sided nature of the victory). That morning, a call came to my office advising that the team was short on players, and required a substitute if I fancied fulfilling the role. They needed somebody who lived close enough to both their office and the Dukes Meadows Sports Ground in Chiswick, where the game would be played, so that they could collect their boots and make it to the ground in time for the 2pm kick-off. This meant an afternoon off work, potentially playing football and being paid for it. It effectively meant

I would be a professional footballer. I was back in Hammersmith, at home picking mud off my boots within minutes of putting the phone down.

When I arrived at the ground and started getting changed, it appeared we were a few men down. Slowly they filtered into the dressing room until finally the captain, Dave Waller, announced we had eleven men in total, and there had been no word from the left-back. There were no mobile phones in 1984, and the carrier pigeons were on strike (everybody seemed to be on strike in 1984), so there was no other option: "Kelvin, can you play left-back?" I just laughed, I'd never played left-back in my life. Of course I couldn't play left-back! That must have given the skipper confidence. My hero, Joey Jones, played that position but I was nothing like him. I weighed nine stone wet through and generally avoided the physical side of the game. I had one tackle in my locker, and I usually kept it in my shorts. I was more your Micky Fillery type, floating around lazily in midfield, delivering a saucy pass to nobody in particular and then spending the next five minutes admiring it, all the while ensuring I didn't have a single hair out of place. I had hair in 1984. Loads of it.

As I lined up on the left of the defence, I suddenly realised I'd forgotten my shin pads. Fortunately, our goalkeeper, an older chap by the name of Hywel, was wearing a pair and said I could borrow them. When he handed them to me I laughed for a second time (not the second time ever, you understand, just the second time since I'd been asked to play left-back. I actually laughed quite a lot when I was younger). What Hywel had handed to me were some pre-war, concertina cardboard efforts that Stanley Matthews might have turned his nose up at. The good news was that if my leg snapped below the knee and above the ankle, I could have just written the address on the shin pad and posted the bottom half of my leg to the hospital. The other positive was that I didn't tackle anyway, so probably wouldn't need them.

After a shaky start, I began to warm to the task. It helped that our opponents had a striker who was at least twice my age and was actually slower than I was in a sprint, which means he was almost certainly the slowest man in the south of England. My confidence soared when he looked odds-on to open the scoring from just a couple of yards out, before I nipped in ahead of him and put the ball out for a corner. A few minutes later I flew into a tackle and missed everything, man and ball, but the fact I had attempted a challenge at all was progress in itself. So I gave myself a metaphorical pat on the back and ensured my hair still looked good, then cracked on with the rest of the game.

The truth is I did OK that day, and I suspect I surprised my team-mates, who had only my previous trial performance to judge me on, even more than I surprised myself. In the second half I actually started to enjoy what I was doing. Our opponents weren't particularly good, and I found myself playing little one-twos out of defence, and making the occasional foray down the wing. Then, with my team two goals to the good, we got a corner on our left. By now starting to play with the swagger of a Maldini, I made a late run forward and as I reached the edge of the penalty area, took a pass direct from the corner-kicker. In my head, the idea was to trap the ball and make an angle for a cross to the far post. Fortunately, as the ball reached me and I saw a row of defenders charging out, the old nerves kicked in and my first touch was so bad that it teed me up for the only option I had left – a shot which sailed over the keeper's head and into something like the top corner of the net.

Cheeky rather than cocky, but in truth possessing levels of self-confidence I would trade a limb for today, I did have a good rapport with my team-mates, who were all generally a bit older than me and seemed to warm to my playful sense of humour. They knew I was desperate to impress, and as they chased after me to give me a celebratory hug, I suddenly found pace I never knew I had. Adrenaline pumping, I was halfway to Hammersmith before they caught up with me. The goal was scored in Chiswick but my triumphant roar could be heard in Chessington, Chesham and Chester. Our big, jovial centre-half Pete Belleone, who was a great guy and always seemed to enjoy my attempts at humour, raced over pointing and guffawing at the audacity of what I had just done, which in turn made me burst out laughing. Even now, almost 40 years later, that moment really makes me happy and brings a little tear to my eye.

We won 4-0 and as we were leaving for home, Dave Waller told me he would be in touch to let me know when the next round would be played. I was in the team – I'd made the left-back spot my own!

It was after Christmas that the date of the next round was known: January 30, 1985. I put it in the diary, it would be another half-day telling myself I was a professional footballer. I would be well in the mood for it that day, too, because two nights prior I would be at Stamford Bridge to watch Chelsea beat Sheffield Wednesday in a League Cup quarter-final game. However, that particular encounter didn't go to plan. The Blues came from behind to draw 1-1, but Kerry Dixon had a penalty saved in the second period which should have eased the passage into the last-four. As it was, we would now face a replay at Hillsborough, on the evening of January 30, 1985!

As we left the Bridge on that Monday night, my two companions – my brother Keith and our mate Steve Kersey – and I discussed the logistics of getting to Sheffield at less than 48 hours' notice. We all had jobs, and one of us had a football match to consider, so it wasn't straightforward, but time was of the essence if we wanted to make arrangements to travel up. Truth be told, I deliberated short and hard, but I always knew I would be going to Hillsborough. I was always going to be at that game, even if I went on my own.

The following day, Keith, Steve and I got our train tickets sorted with

Chelsea, and we were all set to be on the Special out of Kings Cross. I called Dave Waller and told him I was injured and wouldn't make the game. I felt guilty because he'd already had quite a few players cry off, so little old me had become a more important cog in the wheel all of a sudden. That said, little old me was never going to make much difference if the team was already depleted, and that was borne out by the 8-2 defeat they suffered that afternoon.

For me, of course, the rest is history. I got to witness the greatest game I ever saw live. Three down at the break, Paul Canoville joined the fray at half-time in place of the injured Colin Lee, and scored within seconds with his first touch of the ball. Kerry Dixon made it 2-3 midway through the half, before Mickey Thomas levelled the scores with a lovely strike, following great work by Pat Nevin. With five minutes remaining, Canoville scored his second to put Chelsea ahead, and the bundle on the away terrace was incredible. Upwards of six thousand Blues fans had begged, stolen or borrowed to be in Sheffield at such short notice, and that moment alone made it all completely worthwhile for every single one of us.

Some time around 10pm that evening, my voice packed in completely and didn't return for 48 hours. It was an extraordinary night, even if a last-minute penalty and a goalless extra-time period meant a second replay would be required (which we won a week later, courtesy of Mickey T's late, late header on another steamy Stamford Bridge occasion).

If there was a downside to that incredible night, it came with the sight of South Yorkshire Police snatch squads scattering innocent away supporters heading back to the station after the game, and throwing some into their vans to either assault or detain until they'd missed the last train South. We'd stood on the ill-fated Leppings Lane terrace that night, and it was a useful insight into the conduct of that particular police force which would, little more than four years later, become mired in something far worse and far more sinister than we could ever have imagined at the time.

Kelvin Barker has written and co-written several books about Chelsea including the incredibly brilliant 'Celery! Representing Chelsea in the 1980s'. Follow Kelvin on Twitter @neal_army

CHELSEA DOWN UNDER
Ross-John (RJ) Bonaccorsi

After waking up at 3am during my family getaway in Nelson's Bay, New South Wales, I sat up in my bed next to my young son and wife to witness my team Chelsea 'complete football'. Winning the FIFA Club World Cup not only reinforced the Club's status as the best on the planet but more importantly for me capturing that last remaining trophy to complete the set was hugely satisfying.

Moving from the bedroom to the balcony, I had a fresh cup of coffee in hand and smile on my face overlooking the sunrise on a glorious Sunday morning and thought about the long journey it took to be crowned the world's best. More specifically, I reflected deeply on the two-and-a-half-decade-long rollercoaster ride I have sat on as a Chelsea fan and, to put it succinctly, what a ride it's been!

For all of the dizzying heights in terms of trophies won, the derby wins, the records achieved, the milestones celebrated, and the incredible collective and individual moments we have seen, we have equally suffered some bitter lows over the years, including the gut-wrenching last-minute losses and those heart-breaking defeats in finals and semi-finals.

That said, and while it might sound cliché, I sincerely wouldn't change a thing! Sure, some of our success could have been more easily / quickly obtained, but one of the reasons why I love Chelsea so much is because of the character the different squads have shown over the years to overcome adversity and do it the hard way.

With that in mind, I wanted to share my personal reflections on what it's like being a Chelsea fan from 'Down Under' (Australia) and revisit some of my most treasured memories in supporting our Club.

Becoming a Blue

First let's set the scene. Being of Italian heritage, I recall starting to follow the mighty Blues as a young boy in the mid-late 1990s when my fellow Italian contingent of Gianluca Vialli, Roberto Di Matteo, and soon after, Gianfranco Zola joined the Club. Each of these three had a strong presence and influence for Chelsea in their own unique way which I loved, and the trio helped me develop my bond and affinity with Chelsea.

Then at the turn of the millennium, specifically in June 2001, Frank Lampard joined and instantly became my favourite ever Blue and would remain so to this day! Perhaps Frank and I sharing the same birthday, jersey number and position might have had something to do with it, but I like to think that his incredible consistency, professionalism, leadership, personality, his records set and broken, and his role in helping us build an empire were the key contributing factors for my idolising of the man, the myth, the legend that is 'Super' Frank Lampard.

In terms of my 'supporter style', I am someone who watches every match 'live' and have done so for over 20 years. I love to think critically about each game both tactically as well as from a pure enjoyment perspective, including watching each pre and post-match interview to listen carefully to what our players and manager have to say at the time. I also read many articles and listen to/watch a lot of Chelsea podcasts/videos, as well as regularly produce my own Blues and Premier League content.

In short, living and breathing all things Chelsea has become part of my life fabric, perhaps even to the annoyance of those around me!

Being a 'Down Under' Blue

Being born and raised in Sydney can sometimes make following the club a challenging, yet interesting experience. For example, while the time-zone is a naturally obvious factor that comes to mind given Chelsea generally tend to play between 11pm – 5am, and often multiple times a week, strangely that has been something I have become accustomed to since I was a young boy. The only real difference between watching The Blues back then vs now is that instead of waking up / going straight to school, I carry the same sense of sleep deprivation to work and also juggle family and other real-world commitments! Given this, this is where the outcome of watching our games becomes incredibly important for how my day goes!

On one hand, when we win a game, my mood is at an all-time high! Sure, having a few more hours sleep would have been nice, and sure I would feel fatigued and exhausted during the day (despite multiple coffees, plenty of food etc), but, the adrenalin rush I get seeing us claim a victory (even if I am enjoying it via silenced fist pumps in the air while my family are sleeping), makes it well and truly worth it! Occasionally I am able to celebrate these moments with friends at a reasonable hour (11.30pm) or go to a bar with other passionate Chelsea fans and live the action in full voice which is awesome!

On the other hand, when we lose, draw or don't get the result we need, the feeling of utter pain is very real! Not only is sacrificing sleep a decision that I know comes with a cost, but to have it compounded by a poor performance and/or result is like scoring an own-goal and getting injured or injuring a teammate in the process i.e., it's a real double blow! From the physical illness in the pit of my stomach, to the splitting headaches, to the overall sadness experienced for several hours / days, being a Blues fan over the years has certainly increased my levels of stress and put pressure on my life expectancy!

Putting the time-zone challenges to the side is something I have acclimatised to, the most difficult hurdle that I have not quite overcome, but begrudgingly have accepted over the years, is that I am unable to get involved and participate in supporting Chelsea in the way that I know I would had I not lived approximately 17,000 kilometres (10,500 miles) away from Stamford Bridge.

As someone who is highly passionate about supporting my team with other equally-passionate fans, not being able to enjoy that sense of camaraderie and cultural experience to its fullest is something that genuinely hurts. While I love seeing many of my friends that I have been fortunate enough to meet online and regularly chat with experience the pre, during and post-match rituals of each matchday, I wish that I could also be a part of it. Perhaps one day!

To those that go to the games regularly and sing their hearts out with friends and family, and sit on the edge of their seats to cheer on our team throughout at the expense of their voices afterwards, I salute you!

Best moments as a Blue

One of the most difficult questions I sometimes get asked is: *What are some of your favourite highlights as a Chelsea fan?* Fortunately, I've been able to articulate my thoughts on this question in many articles I have written and on podcasts and streams I have appeared on. In truth, while some are forever ingrained in my memory, I will often forget some at the time which I later will remember and wish I mentioned! While being a Blues fan means there's an abundance of glorious moments to celebrate, my overarching answer is that my favourite moment is in 'the moment'. Being able to watch each game 'live' is what I am genuinely grateful for.

Notwithstanding this, some of my more special moments at a macro level are the following:

• Super Frank's double vs Bolton in 2005 to win our first Premier League title in 50 years which signified the beginning of our dynasty.

• Chelsea's 2012 Champions League miracle run. From the Branislav Ivanovic winner against Napoli, to the miracle at the Nou Camp, all the way through to King Didier's late equalising header and winning spot-kick against Bayern Munich in their own backyard to win our first UCL title.

• The highly enthralling Premier League and FA Cup double in 2009-10 under Carlo Ancelotti.

• Chelsea's second Champions League crown whereby the Blues dominated from start to finish. Lampard did a great job in guiding the troops to comfortably topping their group before Thomas Tuchel came in and expertly led them in the knockout stages all the way to lifting the

crown via a 1-0 tactical masterclass against Pep Guardiola's star-studded Citizens in the final.
- Roberto Di Matteo's long-range rocket after 42 seconds which set the tone to help The Blues win the FA Cup 2-0 against Middlesbrough in 1997.
- As mentioned at the start, Chelsea winning the Club World Cup in 2022 to complete the trophy puzzle.

From an actual personal 'live' experience, the two stand-out moments for me are:
- Watching the 2021 Champions League final with hundreds of Blues fans gathered at this bar in Sydney was an amazing experience! We were all singing, chanting, expressing collective gasps and sighs of relief throughout, and of course the place went into pure pandemonium both when Kai Havertz scored and when the final whistle blew!
- Going to see the Blues play live in Sydney in 2015 in a friendly against Sydney FC. A Jose Mourinho-led Chelsea ended up winning 1-0 on the night via a Loic Remy goal but being able to watch some of my heroes in the flesh, including John Terry, Petr Cech, Eden Hazard, Cesar Azpilicueta, Diego Costa, John Obi Mikel and Branislav Ivanovic was a surreal experience in which I will never forget!

On a more micro scale, the following are some of my treasured memories:
- Michael Essien's thunderbolts vs Arsenal and Barcelona at Stamford Bridge. Both different in lots of ways but the commonality they shared was their sheer quality and ferocity. Truly iconic goals that I watch regularly!
- Eden Hazard's solo runs against Arsenal, West Ham and Liverpool. Like a Gianfranco Zola 2.0, our Belgian maestro delivered a mountain of masterclass moments but the above ones in their individual moments at the time were simply breath-taking!
- Speaking of little magicians, the original entertainer for me was my first idol of the club, Gianfranco Zola. The Italian stallion gave us so many amazing memories. However, the two that really stood out for me were his audacious flick from the corner vs Norwich, and, his mesmerising dribble that would forever haunt Liverpool legend Jamie Carragher.
- From a game point of view, the one that I always reminisce about is Chelsea's epic 3-2 victory against Everton when both Super Frank and King Didier scored long-range screamers in the final 10 minutes to seal our come-from-behind win at Goodison Park.
- While Lampard scored some special and hugely important goals for Chelsea, I always love re-watching his turn and volley against Bayern Munich at Stamford Bridge, his scarcely-believable chip from the by-line against Barcelona at the Nou Camp, and, his penalty against Liverpool in

extra time which was emotion-packed given his mother had passed away only a few days earlier. That moment typified the strength and character of Super Frank.

As I said though, while it's wonderful to re-live some of the best memories, it also feels a disservice to the many I haven't listed e.g. Eidur Gudjohnsen's and Olivier Giroud's overhead kicks, Nemanja Matic's rocket vs Tottenham, Reece James' equaliser in the crazy 4-4 against Ajax, the 6-0 thrashing of Arsenal in Wenger's 1000th game in charge of The Gunners. Then there's the return of Lampard as Chelsea manager, an era which, while it ended the way it did, had some amazing memories. The list of magical moments is about as long and impressive as Chelsea's ever-growing trophy cabinet!

Final Thoughts

I am a proud and passionate Chelsea fan from Sydney, Australia that has been a Blue since the mid-late 1990s. I have experienced the highest of highs and lowest of lows in supporting our club, but as the saying goes: It's a Chelsea thing!

While sometimes I see discussions regarding the supposedly different types of Chelsea fans that exist, such as 'international fans', 'matchday going fans', 'legacy fans', 'new fans' etc, my perspective is that this is all irrelevant. Regardless of where you come from, the duration of your support, the motivation for your affinity, the common denominator is that we are all bonded by Chelsea Football Club, and are plain and simply, Chelsea 'fans'!

Here's hoping for many more years of glory and success, and that the heartache we experience along the way is relatively mild and short-lived! Until then, KTBFFH!

RJ Bonaccorsi is ~~an international~~ a Chelsea Fan who blogs and broadcasts passionately about his love for The Blues. Give him a follow on Twitter @RJ_Goodthings

MY FAVOURITE YEAR
Neil Fitzsimon

When the final whistle blew at White Hart Lane on March 14, 1970, after Chelsea's storming 5-1 FA Cup semi-final win over Watford, the joy that my team had reached their second FA Cup Final in three years, soon gave way to my usual bouts of anxiety of, would this be the year that the cup finally came to Stamford Bridge? So many times we'd been the bridesmaids, always seeming to fall at the final hurdle. Worst of all, our last Wembley appearance in 1967 against the hated Spurs, had resulted in a 2-1 defeat for the Blues; a result that was responsible for the festering wound that still exists to this day in Chelsea supporters of a certain vintage.

Now, the other semi-final was between Leeds and Man United, and like most Blues fans, I was hoping that Man United would prevail. Although they possessed the likes of Best, Charlton, and Law, they were, in reality, a team in decline. Leeds, however, were a fearsome prospect at that time. They were most probably the finest club side in Europe in that era. And what's more, they'd destroyed Chelsea at the Bridge back in January when they'd ran out 5-2 winners. It was, indeed, a daunting prospect. True, Chelsea had what was almost certainly at that point, the best side they'd ever had in the club's history. But still, a showdown against Don Revie's formidable Leeds machine was something I didn't fancy at all. Of course, Leeds eventually overcame Man United in a second replay when Billy Bremner's goal took the Yorkshire club to a date with destiny against my beloved Blues on April 11,1970.

During the weeks leading up to the final, I often had a daydream that reoccurred on a regular basis. It went like this:

The game is locked at 2-2 moving into injury time when Leeds' Norman Hunter tries a back-pass near the touchline in front of the Royal Box at Wembley. As the ball arcs through the air, it soon becomes apparent that Hunter's effort has been totally under-hit. Out of nowhere, Chelsea's Ian Hutchinson closes down Leeds keeper Sprake before he can clear the ball. Sprake is still favourite but somehow Hutch manages to block Sprake's attempted clearance. The ball rebounds off Hutch's boot towards the Leeds goal. Now it's a straight race between Hutch and Sprake as to who can get to the ball first. Just as the ball is about to go over the by-line, Hutch stretches out a gangly leg and manages to fire the ball from an oblique angle past the despairing last-ditch attempt by Leeds keeper, Sprake, to block Hutch's shot - an attempt that proves to be fruitless as the ball hits the underneath of the crossbar and bounces down over the line into the unguarded Leeds goal.

Seconds later, amid scenes of jubilation, the ref blows the final whistle and Chelsea have won the cup! I can picture skipper Ron Harris leading the Chelsea players up to the Royal Box to collect the prize that has always eluded the Blues until this glorious moment – the FA Cup! I can see Billy Bremner, the Leeds captain, crying, and their manager Don Revie's face resembling a bulldog chewing a wasp.

Now, this daydream was often broken by firstly, the alarm going off informing me that I had another day at school to endure; secondly, the bus conductor bellowing 'fares please' straight into my ear; or lastly, a piece of chalk hurtling towards me, thrown by a teacher to advise me, not too politely I must add, to stop looking out of the window and instead, concentrate on what God-awful rubbish he or she was droning on about.

Now, here's the strange thing, I had the same dream the other night. It varied not one iota in any way from that same dream I first had over five decades before.

As we all know, in reality Chelsea did lift the Cup for the first time that year after a bruising 2-1 win over dirty Leeds at Old Trafford, but at least part of my dream came true when Hutch saved Chelsea in the first game at Wembley, when his brilliant diving header saved the day with just four minutes remaining, to earn us a 2-2 draw, and the chance of a replay.

Since those epic days, I've been to countless Blues games but somehow, it's always that season of 1969-70 that resonates with me. Why? Who knows? Perhaps it's because I look back on those days as an era of lost innocence or perhaps it's the thrill of going regularly to the Bridge for the first time that season either on my own or with my sister.

I can remember saying to my sister after one home game that season, 'I reckon we're going to win the cup this year,' a comment spoken in hope, yes, but there was also a quiet belief amongst Blues fans, that this Chelsea side had a hardness and resolve to go with the flair, a factor that had been an endemic weakness that had haunted the club for years.

There are two memories I have from that historic season. I can recall with vivid clarity, the home-game at the Bridge in October 1969 against West Brom. It was a beautifully, sunny autumn day. I can remember arriving at Euston as the sunlight dappled through the main concourse of Euston Station. The excitement of reaching London on my own at 14-years of age was a feeling of anticipation mixed with apprehension about how the Blues would get on that day. As it turned out, it was all-in-all a pretty routine win for Chelsea who won the game 2-0, thanks to first-half goals from Ossie and Charlie Cooke. Ossie's header for the first goal that day was a magnificent effort from the edge of the penalty area when he rose majestically to meet Charlie Cooke's pinpoint cross, who himself would go on to score Chelsea's second goal a few minutes later.

TALES FROM THE SHED

I know that this game was on ITV's 'Big Match' the following day, but having trawled through YouTube countless times, I've yet to see any footage. The main reason that game sticks in my memory is because as I was making my way from Euston to Euston Square, which was my preferred route to the Bridge via High Street Kensington, Earls Court and then Fulham Broadway, I noticed a rather tall woman and what I thought was her little boy, approaching the glass door that I was going to exit through. Because my mum had brought me up properly, I opened the door to let the lady and her child through first, only to discover that the child was in fact comedian Ronnie Corbett of 'The Two Ronnies' fame. I did a double take as they walked past me, both thanking me for being so courteous. At that age I was completely star struck as the diminutive Corbett and what I later found out to be his wife, made their way into the station. Now remember, I was only 14-years old but even at that tender age, I towered over little Ronnie. I subsequently discovered that he was a regular visitor to the Bridge which was a plus in his favour in my eyes. On the negative, he also apparently had a soft spot for Crystal Palace which leads me on to the memories of another game I went to that season when the Blues visited Palace on December 27, 1969.

I had been thwarted the day before - yes that's right, the day before - unthinkable in the modern era, that Chelsea had beaten Southampton 3-1 on Boxing Day just 24-hours before they were due to face Palace at Selhurst Park. That game against Southampton was an early kick-off, around 11 o'clock if I remember correctly. After I'd walked the two miles to my local railway station at Apsley that misty Boxing Day morning, I was horrified to find that the station was shut and that there was only a Sunday service which meant that the train I should have been catching had already left Hemel Hempstead railway station, which was a couple of miles away. In a word, I was stranded with nowhere to go.

Disconsolately, I headed for home whereupon I was pressed into action by discovering that the doctor had been round and diagnosed that my mum, who'd been really unwell that Christmas, had come down with pleurisy. My dad, being the eternal opportunist, instructed me to leave immediately on my bike to fill the doctor's prescription at the emergency chemist. All-in-all it had been a very strange day.

Still, I thought, now that I've done my duty as a loving son, and with money saved from my thwarted attempt at attending the Bridge that day, surely my parents would have no objection to my travelling across London to see Chelsea take on Palace the following day, particularly as I'd been given a choice by my parents between Southampton at home or Palace away. So the pendulum had swung back in favour of a trip to Selhurst Park despite my mum and dad's concerns about a long trek across London to an area I knew little about. However, I would take no objection on their part.

Consequently, the next day being the December 27, I found myself on the boneshaker that passed for a railway train that took you from

Victoria to that rather depressing, bleak area of South-East London where Palace had their home. That day I was befriended by a Palace-supporting father and daughter who advised me that it might be a good idea for me to remove my blue and white scarf, as I'd inadvertently wandered into a section of the ground that was full of home supporters. Through the hubris of youth, I totally ignored their advice.

Chelsea looked strangely subdued that day and it was no surprise when Palace took the lead through Gerry Queen's deflected effort that looped over Chelsea keeper, Peter Bonetti. The Palace crowd, who were really getting behind their team, celebrated the opening goal like they'd just won the cup. For me, it was a chastening experience due to the fact that I was surrounded by Palace supporters. I had little choice but to just stand there and take it on the chin. After all, I was just a lone figure in a blue and white scarf amongst a sea of claret and blue.

Now, Palace had taken a point from us following a 1-1 draw back at the Bridge at the beginning of the season. Surely, these newly promoted upstarts were not going to become a bogey side for us. Those fears were dispelled when eight minutes before half-time, Ossie pulled Chelsea level. In the second half Chelsea's superiority started to become evident as the Blues' slick passing game often had the home-side chasing shadows.

With 65-minutes gone, and the game still deadlocked at 1-1, Palace's fortunes crashed down upon them like a roof collapsing, as Chelsea's dominance finally paid off. In those last twenty minutes, Chelsea played some of the best football I've ever witnessed whilst following the club. They literally tore Palace to shreds with Ossie hitting a further three goals to take his tally to four for the afternoon.

The final goal of the game, and perhaps the pick of the bunch, was when Peter 'Nobby' Houseman dived full-length to send his header rocketing past the hapless Palace keeper, John Jackson. Yes, that's right! I've actually witnessed Nobby scoring with a header! And let me tell you, Nobby wasn't exactly renowned for his heading ability. In fact, I wouldn't be surprised at all, if that was the only goal he'd ever scored for the Blues with his nut.

When the final whistle blew on Chelsea's 5-1 demolition of the home-side, I turned around to find that the Palace-supporting father and daughter, had disappeared. I should imagine the prospect of facing some smug little git of a Chelsea supporter, was too much for them to stomach.

The following Saturday, Chelsea were due to face Birmingham in the FA Cup third round at the Bridge. It was the beginning of an odyssey that would ultimately end in glory on April 29, 1970, when the Blues finally lifted the trophy that had always escaped them. And though in recent times, the club's achievements have all but eclipsed that FA Cup triumph of 1970, to those of us who were there in those magical days, that team will always hold a special place in our hearts.

Now, when I mention to younger Blues fans that I was there when we lifted the cup for the first time, or that I was at the Bridge when we overcame Bruges 4-0 after extra-time in what was perhaps one of the greatest nights ever at Stamford Bridge, there is almost a look of envy on the faces of the younger generation of our support. Even though they have known nothing but success in their time following the club, I have a feeling that they would give their right arm to wear the badge of honour that proudly states, 'I was there.'

Neil Fitzsimon is the author of 'Rhapsody in Blue: How I fell in love with the great Chelsea team of the early seventies' and 'A Deeper Shade of Blue: Eddie McCreadie's Blue and White Army and a false dawn'. Find him on Twitter @fitzsimonbrogan

THE SHED AND ME
Cliff Auger

To be honest my first view of The Shed was from the North End of the ground and it didn't really register in the mind of a nine-year-old boy in 1969. I was so enthralled to be watching my heroes in blue that I was happy to be anywhere in the ground. My first few games watching Chelsea were ones where I was taken by my Mum and Dad and after getting off the train at Fulham Broadway the first entrance to Stamford Bridge was for the North End so it made perfect sense for us to go in there. My parents treated it like any other day out that they took me to in London and ham sandwiches and orange squash were always in abundance in the packed lunch my Mum prepared.

The games I went to with my parents early on have really faded in my mind but the last one I went to with them was the Charity Shield game against Everton prior to the start of the 1970/71 season and this is when I became aware of The Shed and the passionate Chelsea supporters that occupied it. Although we still watched the game from the North End, I could see and hear the adulation coming from The Shed especially when the FA cup was paraded round the pitch by the players and it was as if something clicked in my mind that it was The Shed that I wanted to be in the next time I went to Stamford Bridge.

For a now 10-year-old, that next game proved to be a bit problematic as my parents wouldn't allow me to attend games on my own and my Dad now had a job where he had to work on Saturdays thus not allowing him and my Mum to take me. Growing up on a council estate in Southall meant that there was always lots of boys to play football with and this proved to be my saving grace as a few of the older lads were going to Stamford Bridge regularly. After a few weeks of constantly nagging and pleading with my parents to let me go to Chelsea with my friends they finally relented, and after talking to the parents of my friends they let me go.

A whole new experience of going to Stamford Bridge now opened up to me and after meeting up with my mates we got the 207 bus to Ealing Broadway, the District Line train to Earls Court, changing there for the Wimbledon train and as we got off at Fulham Broadway the excitement mounted. This time the entrance to the North End of the ground was ignored and five of us made our way past the Bovril gate and up to the main entrance where we queued to get into The Shed. Once we were through the turnstiles, running up the steps and seeing the lush green grass of the pitch for the first time from that end was the most magical thing I had experienced and I can almost feel the excitement over 50-years later. My first few games in The Shed all really blur together and I struggle to remember who Chelsea played and what the results of the games were, but the experience of being with my mates in there and getting to know the songs, the players chants and jumping up and down to 'Knees up Mother Brown', and of course the sheer joy when we scored, will stick in my mind till the day I die.

Being one of the younger and therefore, smaller persons in The Shed I soon became aware of having to get somewhere on the terrace where I could see the match but still be part of the singing and chanting. Halfway down the terracing was a walkway where you could move across The Shed from one side to another. There was a bigger step up to the terrace in the upper part and a crush barrier ran along the length of the walkway with just enough room for some of us younger fans to stand in front of it where we could have a great view of the game, still be involved in the songs but also protected us from the crowd surges when goals were scored. This became our patch for the first few years of being in The Shed.

The aforementioned 'Knees up Mother Brown' was a popular song in those days although I never knew its relevance and only the 'Chelsea' sung at its end was in support of the team! 'You'll never walk alone' was always sung with scarfs aloft after a Chelsea goal was scored as it was in the majority of grounds across the country, it's strange to think now that a song so associated with Liverpool was sung by every teams supporters. It always stuck in my mind the 'Battersea-Stockwell' to-and-fro chants that reflected areas of staunch Chelsea support. The players songs as the team came onto the pitch before kick off were always loud and proud and the first name was always Peter Bonetti as he took his place in The Shed end goal for the warm up. What a sad day it was when he passed away in 2020 and I will always remember Peter being the first player's name that I ever sung.

During the next few seasons, if I had a bit of extra money, I sometimes paid extra to transfer from The Shed into the small area of terracing that used to be in front of the old East Stand, a few of us would go in there and climb on top of the small building that housed the turnstile entrance to watch the game from an elevated position. We often got told off by the people in the East Stand seats for impairing their view of the game!

It was always The Shed that I watched the vast majority of games from and with that there sometimes came trouble! At home to West Ham in 1973, a 13-year-old me came running up The Shed stairs as normal only this time being confronted by an older, bigger West Ham fan draped in a Union Jack flag inviting me to "Come on then, mate!" Discretion being the better part of valour, I promptly returned rather hastily down the stairs again. Thankfully, as more Chelsea supporters entered the ground I was able to return up the stairs and a watch the game all be it with a sizeable amount of West Ham fans remaining in The Shed for the game with a lot of police officers in among them! A few further encroachments of The Shed by opposition fans happened in future years, predominantly West Ham and Millwall, but as the years went on and Chelsea supporters became stronger and more organised the opposition fans were soon 'removed!'

Towards the end of the 1972/73 season, one game that I will always remember was against Manchester United. This was to be the last game that Bobby Charlton played and as much as we all disliked Man Utd there was no getting away from the fact that Charlton was one of the best English players ever and on a highly emotional day he was presented with a memento by the Chelsea chairman, Brian Mears and his name was sung loudly by the entire Shed as he left the pitch at the end of the game. To this day I'm pretty sure that this is the only time that I have ever heard Chelsea supporters sing the name of an opposition player who had never played for our club.

As the years went by it was sad to see The Shed terrace gradually eroding and a part of it having to be sectioned off as it was deemed no longer safe to use. After watching hundreds of games from all areas of the end, The White Wall, The Middle, The Tea Bar, down the front and over by the West Stand, it was a sad day when it was used as a terrace for the last time in 1994.

Happily, I continued to watch games from The Shed after the terraces were demolished when a temporary seating stand was built and then when the newly built stand was completed I was able to take both my sons in the purposely built family section in The Shed Lower and then when they were older to the seats we still have in The Shed Upper. Although The Shed will never be the place it once was its nice at last to be able to use the toilets without paddling in pee and to get something to eat and drink that doesn't risk salmonella poisoning!

Efforts have been made over the last few years to get the atmosphere better in The Shed and it has worked well at times. It's also great to see banners for players from the era when I started watching Chelsea, Ossie, Tambling, Bonetti, being displayed in the area of the ground that idolised them. It's not just players that are honoured either as one of Chelsea's finest supporters, Mick Greenaway, having a banner on the back wall of The Shed Upper.

Although The Shed is not the end it once was, it's still a real shame that it has to be shared with away supporters and I really hope in the future, whether the stadium remains the same or is rebuilt entirely, that it returns to being for Chelsea supporters only and becomes, once again, the spiritual home end of Stamford Bridge.

Cliff Auger is the Chairman of the Chelsea Supporters' Trust and also coordinates regular matchday collections for the Hammersmith and Fulham Foodbank. Follow Cliff on Twitter @MIBIAL

BACK TO THE KING'S ROAD
Daniel Childs

Never had I felt such pulsating excitement for a match like this. My eyes widened, any sense of grogginess was nowhere to be found - all I could think was, it was Cup Final day! So much so that I had to vocally say it to my Mum: "It's Cup Final day!" I had only found out a couple of weeks before the final that I would be going and like the lead up to Christmas I was counting down the days.

My pristine yellow Adidas away shirt was ready to go, and a pair of cameo shorts given I was big into wrestling at the time and idolised John Cena. This game for me felt different to others, almost a coming of age in a sense and a chance to experience what previous generations of my family had supporting Chelsea on a major cup final day. It was May 30, 2009, and Chelsea were playing Everton in the FA Cup Final at Wembley. I was at the 2007 final when Didier Drogba had prevented Manchester United's 'double' and turned the rebuilt stadium's arch blue, as the old one had been before.

Personally, at the age of nine, seeing us win the FA Cup for the first time in my life ranks as my favourite match-going experience. I wasn't in Munich nor Porto, so the noise of our end when Drogba's goal hit the net remains top and I can still visualise a sea of blue descending into bedlam. But what stands out about the final that followed it two years later was the madness, fear, chaos, unity and triumph that befell a pretty ridiculous day.

What made the game specifically unique to me was the idea of riding an open-top bus from West London to Wembley. The sun was shining. Me, my older Brother and Grandad all arrived early at Nine Elms Fruit and Veg Market and soon there were many "Carefrees" to be had. Through central London, past Big Ben with a bit of "Oh Dennis Wise" as some home-made Samosa's were passed round which are still the greatest I've ever tasted. It was like Chelsea's greatest hits being played with the backdrop of glistening London views as we got closer to Wembley and the arch came into view. I had been told the stories from my Dad, uncles and grandparents of previous bus trips to FA Cup finals, be that Middlesbrough in 1997, Villa in 2000 and Arsenal in 2002 and for me this was my first taste.

As we approached Wembley we were expecting to arrive at the Chelsea end of the ground where the bus would park and we would have some food before the game. Unexpectedly, for whatever maddening reason that I still haven't got any closer to understanding 13-years later, our driver drove us to the Everton end! The only way I can describe the picture of a thousand Evertonians seemingly turning towards our bus was like a scene out of 'The Walking Dead'. With a Chelsea flag hanging over the front and the majority of us in London blue, there was no chance we'd go unnoticed. Our bus soon became target number one for missiles. Full beer cans were flung from several directions smacking the side panels and each thud seemed to get increasingly louder and more vicious. We started singing "Carefree" in defiance but a day that had started with excitement was now brim-full with fear and panic. My brother covered me up with a flag but this wasn't enough to prevent a full can hitting me on the head. The driver, realising his mistake, changed direction but we were moving so slowly through this barrage of animosity that I thought it was never going to end. Eventually we got to our end and my panic was soothed by the sounds of "Chelsea, Chelsea, Chelsea" coming from outside our bus. Although shaken, by some miracle no one got seriously injured and we enjoyed some food under the arch.

The final itself was equally chaotic as Louis Saha broke Roberto Di Matteo's cup final record by scoring within 25-seconds. But now in reflection, it was never in doubt with Didier Drogba and Frank Lampard both on the pitch. Sat in the lower tier and seeing in front of my eyes, my hero Super Frank scoring one of our greatest cup final goals still feels like a fantasy.

One of my defining memories from the end of the game was the Chelsea crowd urging caretaker-coach Guus Hiddink to stay on after doing such a fine job in challenging circumstances. How many of us could have predicted he would be back six years later to take up an identical interim position. A classy man who served an almost selfless role in wait for a title-winning Italian to replace him for the following season.

Then as the confetti had covered the Wembley turf and the playlist of our favourite songs ended after the trophy lift, we were back outside in the early evening sun to enjoy some more food and drinks. The most edgy thing my 11-year-old self could think of was drinking Red Bull which ensured I didn't sleep later that night. Why did I need to? Chelsea had just won the cup.

The highlight of this trip was the slow drive back to the King's Road as we entered the London evening. Now the roles were reversed as we left Wembley, the surrounding area contained sparsely populated Everton fans making their long trips home. One flinging a can towards us, completely missing and then him being covered in beer himself, head down and dejected as we laughed hysterically. Just like before it was the same ritual of us all going through the Chelsea hymn sheet one by one. From Wembley, through Shepherd's Bush and then to the glorious borough of Kensington and Chelsea. Every time a Chelsea car passed with a flag attached we would cheer loudly as they honked their horns. Being a young kid it felt like we were experiencing our own victory parade as our boisterous noise attracted the attention of mostly confused bystanders who looked on with interesting expressions.

Finally we arrived to the glory of the King's Road – home!

Daniel Childs is a writer and presenter for 'football.london' and also presents shows on his popular YouTube channel 'Son Of Chelsea'. Follow Daniel on Twitter @SonOfChelsea

PRICEY BUT NICE
Clayton Beerman

The sky was black... the rain had come as we left the FA Cup Final in 1994. We had just been beaten 4-0 by a combination of Manchester United and referee David Elleray. We didn't deserve to get such a hammering and to get rained on added insult to injury. We were so excited that day to be finally back at Wembley but alas it was not to be.

As we trudged back to the car, we saw some United fans. They were minding their own business and showing no visible signs of having just won a trophy we were desperate for. One of our party started shouting at them in frustration asking why they weren't celebrating. All these years later it is evident that winning that trophy is never as good as the first time. You see United were in the middle of wonderful streak of winning silverware. They had won the League the week before and the FA Cup was the cherry on top and they were used to winning everything.

So why am I bringing this up? Whenever Chelsea fans are asked what was better, winning the League at Bolton in 2005 or winning the Champions League in Munich in 2012 it is almost impossible to respond. Winning the League became inevitable because of the season we'd had, but the joy of that day was something to behold. Winning in Munich was the complete opposite, we had no hope or so many thought. I was lucky enough to be at both games and if I had to choose today which was the best experience I would say Bolton... but ask me tomorrow and the answer might be different. Both victories were the first time for me and in the case of the Champions League for the Club as well and as I have already said it's never as good as the first time.

When I was growing up the actual thought of us winning either of those trophies was incomprehensible. Throughout the 1970s and 1980s English teams reigned supreme in Europe. We won the now defunct Cup Winners' Cup in 1971 but then disappeared without trace. It was an age where football fans followed and cheered on every British success. Year-after year in Europe it was either Liverpool or Nottingham Forest or Aston Villa or Everton picking up silverware. At home it was the same and then the domination of Manchester United and Arsenal started. We were a cup team for the large part at the end of the 1990s and beginning of the 2000s.

The League wasn't something that Chelsea came really close to winning in my time of supporting the Club until 1999. We were an attractive team playing fantastic football and were handily placed in the table and had a home game against Leicester City who had nothing to play for. If you mention the name Steve Guppy, most Blues supporters know the rest. Thanks to Gianfranco Zola and Dan Petrescu we were 2-0 up with eight minutes to go but then Michael Duberry scored an own-goal and with just two minutes left Foxes winger Steve Guppy curled the ball beyond Ed De Goey into the net and the title was blown. I remember watching the game in a bar in Majorca. After the final whistle, me and the same shouty mate who had been with me at the 1994 Wembley debacle just wandered over the road to the beach and stared out to sea for what seemed like ages. It wasn't what ultimately cost us glory but it was just the way things were. We didn't win leagues. That season we finished four points behind Manchester United who knew how to cross the line.

The 2004 season saw the arrival of the Special One. That season was as good as it gets. We were very good and there was to be no Steve Guppy moments. The charge to the title was in hindsight relentless. We went to games expecting to win, a very strange sensation. As the season progressed, the moment we took the lead that was it, the game was done. Our rivals, principally Arsenal, were beginning to disintegrate under the pressure. Notwithstanding all of this I still couldn't believe we were actually going to win the League.

All that changed on the April 2, 2005. We were playing away at Southampton, we were 2-0 up in the first-half and looking comfortable for another victory. Depending on other results we getting to being single digit points away from winning the title. Then the chant started. "49 years the time has come," and so it went on. Not very catchy, but accurate it was sung for what seemed like ages. I was getting goosebumps and thinking it's really happening. We won 3-1 and we were nearly there.

Just in case I was getting too excited in true Chelsea style we drew our next two games at home, equaling our longest winless streak that season. Then on Saturday, April 30, 2005, we were playing Bolton Wanderers away. I was still an away season ticket holder so tickets were not a problem for arguably the biggest game in the Club's history.

We arrived in Bolton at about lunchtime. As was our tradition we found a nice out of town pub and had lunch and a few drinks to steady the nerves. The Trotters ground, called the Reebok Stadium at that time, was still relatively new but I had been there before. The place was buzzing. Our seats were near the back of the stand, not great but we were privileged to be in. There would be thousands of Chelsea fans who would have wanted to be where I was that day.

The first-half was tough, remarkable as it may seem now, Bolton were a very good side, well managed by Sam Allardyce. We had to defend well and, as always, we were aided by a legend in the making, Petr Cech. There were a few nerves around notwithstanding the fact Chelsea still had several games to play to secure the title but we hoped (albeit didn't say it out loud) that we would win it on the day.

As always Bolton were a tough opponent and we had to wait until the 60th minute for a moment that is now one of the most iconic in the Club's history. A scrappy goal in some respects but Frank Lampard's control and eye for goal was brilliant as always. It is also a little remembered fact that between this goal and the second goal, Petr Cech made a quite brilliant save from a misplaced header by teammate Geremi!. We only had to wait 16 minutes for the second goal. A break led by Claude Makalele and Lampard rounded Bolton keeper Jussi Jaaskelainen for his and Chelsea's second goal. We went mad, we knew our time had come.

At the final whistle tears flowed. Much of what followed was a blur. No trophy celebrations but the players spent what seemed like ages in front of the fans spraying champagne on everyone including Chelsea owner Roman Abramovich. The home crowd stayed and looked on in wonderment and envy no doubt. I am always amazed when fans watch opposing fans celebrate. There was however a curious bond between Chelsea and Bolton Wanderers supporters which went back to a match at Stamford Bridge between the teams in May 1998. It was the last game of the season and either Bolton or Everton would get relegated. Blues fans sided with Bolton on the day to the extent that there was mock booing when Gianluca Vialli opened the scoring in the 73rd minute. Chelsea went on to win 2-0 and sadly Bolton went down but obviously our 'support' for them was forgotten as our title win at The Reebok was warmly welcomed by their fans. Their vehement dislike of neighbours Manchester United probably also had something to do with it.

(Editor's note: Given that Chelsea legend Frank Lampard is currently the Everton manager, should this scenario replicate itself during his tenure as Toffees boss it would be interesting to see which team Blues fans would align themselves with.)

Eventually, we reluctantly left the stadium to go back to the car. After the final whistle we'd decided we would stay the night in Bolton as the celebrations had to continue with more drinks on the menu so we made our way back to the pub that we'd drank in before the game. On the way there I phoned home… my wife had plonked my two-year old son in front of the TV to watch the win. I bemoaned the fact it had taken me my whole life to witness Chelsea winning the League. My son had done it within 24 months!!!

One of our group got on very well with the pub's landlady who helped with the Yellow Pages (a telephone directory for the younger readers!). A hotel was booked and off we went. The first question we asked on arrival were details of the best Chinese restaurant in Bolton, the second question was for a taxi to take us there. We piled into the taxi and asked the driver what the restaurant was like. In the broadest Lancashire accent came the immortal words (to us anyway), "Pricey but nice".

We had a great meal and loads more beers. A lot of reminiscing about the truly awful times and lots of laughs. We went back to the hotel to be greeted by a local wedding reception which was straight out of a Peter Kay sketch show. The day and subsequent night were written in my Chelsea folklore. It really was the most incredible occasion and it took a while to sink in that we had actually won the League. The rest, as they say, is history and it has been the most amazing journey. Yes, the last 20-plus years have been amazing but the previous years were equally good in their own way. Following the club I love, making lots of friends and memories... there are plenty of other stories, but Bolton will always be special.

Longstanding Chelsea season ticket holder and scribe for the 'cfcuk' fanzine, Clayton Beerman is the author of 'Palpable Discord: A year of drama and dissent at Chelsea'. Follow him on Twitter @goalie59

BUYING A MAC FOR MOSCOW
Jason Gibbins

It's February 2010. It's November 2009. It's October 2011. It's January 2012. It's March 2014, it's September 2013; it's any other bleak autumn or winter date from 2008 onwards.

And it's cold, and it's dark, and it's pissing down.
And I'm standing impatiently in a park - hat pulled down, collar pulled up - as my dog completes its early-morning ablutions.
And as it does so, I'm picturing John Terry.
I'm picturing John Terry stepping from the centre circle.
I'm picturing John Terry tugging at his left sleeve, rearranging his captain's armband, walking towards Edwin van der Sar.
I'm picturing John Terry's rain-soaked shirt and saying out loud, to no-one in particular, "take it in, take it in, remember everything, savour the moment…"
And then I'm remembering John Terry taking three steps to strike the ball.
And then I'm remembering the split-second of silence as John Terry slips.
And then I'm remembering the despairing disbelief as John Terry's kick strikes the post.
And then I'm remembering the haunted eyes of all those around me.
And then I'm remembering the thunder-clap of United celebration rolling down the stadium.
And then I'm remembering the Mancunian roar washing over me, punching me in my sickened stomach as it goes.
And then I'm looking down at the dog, his clueless dark eyes looking back, and I'm saying 'that was your bloody fault'.

But first came May 1, 2008, the day after Chelsea had booked their place in their first European Cup final, to be held in the Luzhniki Stadium, Moscow. I'd already decided I wasn't going to Moscow. Of course I wasn't going to Moscow. There'd be no change from a grand for a 3,000-mile day trip, and I had two primary school kids I could barely afford to feed. In no sane world could I justify chucking a thousand notes at a day-trip to Moscow. But in the following days it didn't stop me throwing childish sulks because I wasn't going to Moscow. It didn't stop me checking the internet every hour of every day, looking for a bargain flight to Moscow via Helsinki, or Tallinn, or Riga, or Minsk. And when I got home from work a week before Moscow, it didn't stop me thinking Mrs G must be on the ultimate wind-up when she asked me a question about Moscow.

"Do you really want to go to Moscow?" she said.
"Don't take the piss," I said.
"Because I've been thinking," she said.
"What about?" I said.
"I think you should go…" she said.
"Behave," I said.
"But I want something in return," she said.
"I did that last night," I said.
"Don't be crude," she said.
"What then?" I said.
"I want a dog," she said.
"You want a what??" I said.

So that's why, five minutes later - before she could change her mind, before I could change my mind - I was booking a flight to Moscow in exchange for a thousand quid I hadn't got. And that's why, two days later, I was collecting a one-year-old Scottie named Mac in exchange for another three-hundred quid I hadn't got. And that's why every time I walked Mac in the rain… one year later, two years later, or another eight or nine years down the line… my bastard brain always took me back to John Terry's tears and a night of exhausting pain.

It's now about noon, local time, on Wednesday, May 21, 2008; Mac's settling in to his new home, and I'm on a Chelsea flight coming into land at Moscow's Vnukovo Airport. I'm travelling on my own with the hope of meeting my mates later. We'd all cracked at different times, booked at different times and are flying into Moscow from different airports at different times. 'We'll find each other when were there', we'd all said, making only the vaguest of arrangements.

It's now about 2pm local time and I'm walking into Red Square, already wet from a grey cloak of rain covering the city. There's St Basil's Cathedral. There's Lenin's Mausoleum. And there's the GUM shopping arcade with its grand façade and elegant glass roof, selling the wares of Cartier, Gucci and Prada to Russia's new super rich. And there's Paul, standing in the rain, making good on our half-arsed plans to try to meet in the square whenever we arrive. He's a top man Paul, and we laugh at the stupidity of it all; looking at our surroundings and wondering how the hell we are here, how the hell Chelsea – our Chelsea – are in Moscow for the biggest club game in world football?

We head out of the square and Paul guides me to the others who have already arrived – a collection of Chelsea mates picked up along the long road from Division Two. They're bemoaning the lack of obvious drinking options on the wide boulevards surrounding Red Square, so we head beneath the road to buy cans at a small stall hidden in an underpass wall.

One of the group decides he also wants a chocolate bar that he can see on a counter but is out of reach.

"Bounty," he says, to a bemused shrug of the shoulders from the Russian gatekeeper.

"Bounty," he repeats just a little louder, "BOUNTY..."

And eventually, following a confused pause, she responds: "Bounty, Bounty..."

She has no idea what she's just done.

"Bounty, Bounty, Bounty, Bounty la, la, la, la, la..." we all sing on cue as we jump around laughing like drains, "Bounty, Bounty, Bounty, Bounty la, la, la, la, la..."

To be fair, you probably had to be there. But we drink the beers and we walk on, and finally we find a small bar containing a small collection of United fans. I hate United. I've hated them since they beat us in the FA Cup Final in 1994. I've hated them even more since they beat us in the FA Cup semi-final in 1996. But we find a shared bond with the few of their fans drinking outside the bar; a shared respect for all finding a way to Moscow against the financial odds. They're just like us, at the end of the day. They just walk a bit different.

We share drinks, we share stories, we exchange songs, and we all take the piss when Kirk from 'Coronation Street' – the bluntest fictional tool in the Weatherfield box – ambles past us down the street.

"Kirk from Corrie is a w*nker, is a w*nker; Kirk from Corrie is a w*nker, is a w*nker..."

He takes it in good spirits and laughs as he goes, but then the mood starts to change. More United turn up and our small band of Chelsea is now significantly outnumbered. The new arrivals don't share the same goodwill, and there's a new edge to the drinking on the street outside the bar.

And then a beer is thrown in our direction.

And one of our group tries to react.

And as we pull him back we decide it's time to walk away.

It's now 6pm, still nearly five-hours to kick-off; a kick-off time set for the convenience of Western European television audiences, not the thousands who have spent thousands to attend in person. We want to find more Chelsea fans but have no real idea where to look. Moscow is a fascinating city but not a football-friendly city, lacking any obvious places to gather such as those bar-lined squares so loved by English fans abroad. So instead we decide to head to the ground early and drop down into the gloriously ornate Moscow metro system with its marble walls and chandeliers.

Jumping on a train we sing the 'Kalinka', the Russian folk song adopted by the Chelsea faithful in honour of their oligarch owner Roman Abramovich. From its slow start we build the rhythm as our train gathers speed on the tracks... louder, quicker, louder, quicker as we race beneath Moscow; the local commuters looking as confused as they are entertained. It's now 7pm and we step out of Sportivnaya station and, to my delight, there he is, there's Scott. Our phones haven't been working and we haven't been able to make contact, and I was fearing I wouldn't be able to find my best mate on this day of all days. But meeting him is a good sign. It's a sign that gives me hope.

We walk down some side streets and I buy a meat-filled pastry from a street stall. I don't know what the meat is, I don't think I want to know, but after two mouthfuls it's in the bin. But despite meeting Scott the day is still lacking a spark. Everything is too big, everything too wet, everything too closely guarded by Russian military to create an atmosphere worthy of the occasion.So we walk towards the stadium, where we are photographed by Moscow media beneath a statue of Lenin. For their benefit we sing a song about Chelsea winger Solomon Kalou, a song that honours his role in a Liverpool semi-final goal that was crucial to our final progression.

"He comes from the Ivory Coast, his name's Kalou, Kalou;
"He don't take coke like Adrian Mutu, Mutu;
"He crossed the ball from the left, he put the ball on Riise's head;
"AND THAT'S WHY WE LOVE SOLOMON KALOU;
"La la la la la la la la la laaa la la...."

We are trying to enjoy it, trying to get in the mood, but as the clock ticks past 9pm it feels like forced fun. European Cup finals shouldn't be forced fun. Especially when they cost you a grand... And now it's 9.45pm, an hour until kick-off, and I'm queuing at the turnstiles. It's been a *good* day rather than a *great* day, but that doesn't matter now... it's the events of the next 3-4 hours that will be the ultimate judge and juror on how it is remembered.

And so we fast-forward four hours... And it's approaching 2am on Thursday, May 22 following a toe-to-toe 1-1 draw that went to extra time and penalties. It has been the longest night of the longest day. And Manchester United are European Champions. There was still hope when John Terry missed his penalty but, at the same time, there was no hope at all. With that miss, the dream died.

Anderson and Giggs scored sudden-death penalties for United while Kalou prolonged the agony for Chelsea, but then Nicolas Anelka's weak shot was saved by van der Sar and another red roar rolled down the stadium to ram home the final fatal wound.

I walk out of the ground and into the rain; the colour washed from my cheeks and the spirit sucked from my soul. It is another seven hours before I finally find a seat on a flight home, unprepared and unwilling to begin the process of getting on with life... the daily routine of eat, sleep, work, repeat. But time passes by and the misery of Moscow fades, only ever coming back into focus when I walk the dog in the rain.

And then, in the blink of an eye, it's August 14, 2017. About 11am local time.

It's not raining; it's a beautiful warm day and there's not a cloud in the sky.

But I'm again picturing John Terry stepping from the centre circle.

I'm again picturing John Terry tugging at his left sleeve, rearranging his captain's armband, walking towards Edwin van der Sar.

I'm again picturing John Terry's rain-soaked shirt and saying out loud, to no-one in particular, "take it in, take it in, remember everything, savour the moment…"

And then I'm looking down at the dog, his lifeless body placed next to a freshly-dug hole, and I'm saying 'thank you'.

I'm fighting back tears as I lay him to rest, but I'm saying 'thank you, thank you for everything'.

I bought a Mac for Moscow… and it was the best £1,300 I've ever spent.

Jason Gibbins first book, 'For Better Or Worse: Life, love and supporting Chelsea in the 1990s', is scheduled for publication by Gate 17 in 2022. You can follow him on Twitter @Jgibbins

THE PLAYERS' LIFTS LEAGUE
David Johnstone

Whilst many people have, over years, regularly seen the 'cfcuk' Chelsea fanzine sellers hawking their goods out of Sainsbury's carrier bags, what most people fail to appreciate is the headaches that the logistics involved in getting every new issue to our 'home base' - the 'cfcuk' stall on the Fulham Road.

If the game is on a Sunday, Mark 'Marco' Worrall - the editor of 'Tales From The Shed' and regular contributor of articles for the 'cfcuk' fanzine - will journey over to West London and collect me and the fanzines which usually number between 1200 and 1500 copies depending on how many matches the issue is covering.

If the publication date falls on a Saturday or even on a day between Monday and Friday, I call upon the services of a local taxi firm to transport me and 'cfcuk' to Fulham Broadway.

However, on one particular Saturday back in the day, I was pot-less, boracic lint, skint and couldn't afford the price of a taxi so I was forced to get to Fulham Broadway using public transport. It was a struggle. I had two Sainsbury's 'bags for life', each holding two hundred copies of 'cfcuk' as well as a backpack in which I'd managed to cram another 450. The combined weight of these 850 fanzines made it really hard work getting from a-to-b and, by the time I'd negotiated the stairs at Putney railway station (this was in the days before there was a lift), I was sweating.

Literally waddling out of the station, I headed for the Number 14 bus stop across the road, the said route being ideal to drop me off right opposite the location of the 'cfcuk' stall. However, as I began the cross the thoroughfare, a familiar face was staring at me from the driving seat of an Aston Martin DB9. It was Petr Cech, the Chelsea and Czech Republic goalkeeper. I'd known Petr almost from the first day he'd arrived at Chelsea and, indeed, I'd interviewed him for 'The Special Ones', John King and Martin Knight's book celebrating Chelsea's 2005 Premiership Title win.

As I nodded back in recognition at the shot-stopper, he gesticulated that he'd give me a lift in his car. Buoyed by my good fortune, my renewed strength saw me negotiate the traffic which, fortunately for me, was snarled up and as I reached the passenger side of Petr's car, he leant over, opened the door and I managed to squeeze into the seat beside him.

'Packed in like sardines' didn't come close as the two Sainsbury's bags and the backpack combined were both pressing me backwards into the seat and were tight against the windscreen. Nevertheless, the journey to Fulham Broadway was made without incident as Petr chatted to me about his life as the Chelsea goalkeeper. Stopping opposite my stall, the look of disbelief on Marco's face was coupled with laughter as he saw me extract myself from the car. As I thanked Petr profusely and bade him farewell, little did he realise that he had become the first participant of what, that day, became the 'Players' Lifts League'.

In the days before the now common practice of the players staying in a hotel local to Stamford Bridge the night before home matches, those squad members who lived in the Cobham / Oxshott area would drive to Stamford Bridge along Putney High Street and would arrive between three-and-a-half to four hours before a game.

I got into the habit of waiting in the same spot where Petr had picked me up and cadging lifts off the players who would be regularly caught in the usual traffic jam which was a frequent occurrence in that part of Putney. As with Petr, the Chelsea squad knew who I was due in part to the fact that I was working at the Club but also because of the 'cfcuk' fanzine so for them, it was no problem to stop and give me a lift.

As soon as I got into whoever's car I was travelling in, I'd call or text Marco to let him know who I was with in order that he too could acknowledge their kindness as well as seeing the relief on the said player's face that the 'cfcuk' stall was there and still going strong.

Over the years, I was fortunate - rather the players themselves were fortunate - to participate in the Players' Lifts League and the list of those who entered includes the following; Michael Essien, Mikel John Obi, Gary Cahill, Ross Turnbull, Fernando Torres, Paulo Ferreira, Michael Ballack, Henrique Hilário along with both Joe Cole and Frank Lampard, the pair being good enough to give me a lift back to London on a couple of occasions that I found myself at the Cobham training facility.

However, the King of the Players' Lifts League and winner for three consecutive seasons was none other than John Terry who was kind enough to stop and ferry me to the Fulham Road more than any other player.

One story that I know is one of Mark's favourites is the one involving Yuri Zhirkov:

Caught in the traffic, I walked up to Yuri's car and, politely tapping on the passenger door window, I gesticulated with my thumb in the classic hitchhiking way. At first, Yuri - who'd only been at Chelsea a number of weeks - looked nervous and shook his head as he refused. Nevertheless, I persisted and eventually the Russian agreed and opened the door and I jumped into his BMW.

Having only been in England a short time, his conversational English was not the best but, that said, it was far better than my spoken Russian. As we made our way towards Fulham, he told me several stories including how he, along with the 2008 Euros Russia squad, their manager being Guus Hiddink, had been present at the Chelsea v

TALES FROM THE SHED

Manchester United Champions League Final at the Luzhniki Stadium, the then home of Spartak Moscow.

As we got close to where I wanted to be dropped off, I told Yuri a bit about myself and mindset of the Chelsea supporters, including the following, "Some people collect match programmes, some people collect players' autographs but me, I collect lifts from the players…" With pausing and, albeit with a heavy Russian accent but in the best English he'd spoken for the whole journey, Yuri replied, "I know… I saw John Terry pick you up last week…"

Nowadays, as I intimated previously, the players no longer travel to home matches on the day of the game but, should they ever go back to doing so - 'trust me I'm a Chelsea Supporter' the Players' Lifts League will make a long-awaited comeback.

David Johnstone is the proprietor and editor of the 'cfcuk' fanzine which is available to buy at every Chelsea game (home and away) throughout the season and costs only £1 (Hurry Up!). Subscriptions, hard copy and digital, can be purchased online. For further information email fanzine@cfcuk.net

FUTURE LEGENDS
John King

There is something extra-special about a homegrown player breaking into the first team, something extra-exciting about a side loaded with footballers who have come through the ranks, but it has been a long time since Chelsea boasted such a line-up. For years, John Terry stood alone, and if anyone needs proof of the extra qualities such a player can bring they only need to look at our Captain, Leader, Legend. But the last few seasons have seen some positive changes, with several youngsters making their mark, an injection of soul to go with the endless trophies and glory.

A refusal to promote homegrown talent has been a long-term problem in the Premier League, with clubs preferring to buy ready-made stars than develop their own, a short-term approach wrapped up in a craving for instant success and quick profits. Coupled with an obsession for foreign imports, it was tough for local lads trying to make it in the game, the problem so bad that not long ago there was a shortage of top-flight players eligible for the England side. And yet now the squad is overflowing with options, something which is being repeated in Wales and Scotland.

This represents a big shift in attitudes and hasn't happened overnight, but at the same time maybe reflects the wider world, where the masses are rebelling against globalisation and Big Money, looking instead to localism and the need to protect their own cultures. Whatever the reason, at club level Chelsea are up there with the best of them in terms of their youth, although whether the progress made can be maintained after the departure of Frank Lampard remains to be seen.

The first Chelsea team I followed included six homegrown players in Peter Osgood, Alan Hudson, Peter Bonetti, Ron Harris, John Hollins and Peter Houseman. They were born in Windsor, Chelsea, Putney, Battersea, Guildford and Hackney respectively, so three came from within walking distance of Stamford Bridge, two from towns to the West and South-West of London, with only Chopper born on the other side of the city. This localism wasn't unique at the time, as the whole idea of a football club – named after cities and towns – was rooted in location and community. And a few years earlier, Jimmy Greaves, Bobby Tambling and Terry Venables would also have been on that list.

For me, this is the greatest Chelsea side thanks to the Holy Trinity of Osgood, Hudson and Charlie Cooke, flamboyant characters on and off the pitch who set the club apart from the machine-like Leeds and

Liverpool. These two represented the Grim North, but while they had Norman Hunter and Tommy Smith, us Soft Southern shandy-drinkers had the likes of Ronald Harris and David Webb, with the rest of the team happy to get stuck in and fight for their right to entertain.

Manchester United were the self-proclaimed 'Cock Of The North', the Northern version of the 'Pride Of London' – Chelsea FC – and they had a similar homegrown quota in George Best, Bobby Charlton, Brian Kidd, Nobby Stiles, David Sadler, John Aston. George Best – like Robert Chelsea Moore at West Ham – was reportedly keen to play for us, to join up with Osgood, Hudson and Cooke, and later in life he would live near the Kings Road. Bobby Moore liked a drink as well, and if Best and Moore had linked up with Chelsea's finest the pubs would have struggled to cope.

For me, again, that Chelsea team and the football world of the day shaped everything that followed. Chelsea are richer and more successful today, but the essential nature of the club remains the same, thanks to the support and stadium, but also through the traditions passed down across the generations by the players. Their role is of course vital, particularly those who come through the ranks or arrive from outside and fall in love with the club and make it their own. There is still the flamboyance and unpredictability of the Osgood-Hudson era, an ability to make supporters of the duller teams very jealous and even bitter.

While this brilliant Chelsea side went into decline after the FA Cup and Cup Winners Cup victories of 1970 and 1971, the greatest homegrown side of all was forming behind the scenes. The first hint came when Eddie McCreadie took over for the last few games of the 1974/75 relegation season. Ray Wilkins was made captain for the key match at Tottenham, with John Sparrow, Teddy Maybank and Ian Britton also playing alongside Gary Locke, Micky Droy, Harris, Hollins and Ian Hutchinson. The team still included lots of former youth-team players – Droy and Hutchinson were signed from non-league clubs – but the new breed would soon take up all but one of the eleven positions.

Two seasons later Chelsea bounced back in style with a team made up of Chelsea supporters. The Shed was right there on the pitch wearing the shirts. This has to be the best ever season for me, recorded brilliantly in 'Eddie Mac Eddie Mac', while the event held at Stamford Bridge to celebrate the book's release (May 20, 2017) brought home just how close the team and the supporters were at that time. We were essentially the same people. It was an emotional evening, representing everything that is good about Chelsea and football.

Youth team players continued to come through in the years that followed, but it was never the same. In different circumstances Clive Walker and Micky Fillery might have become England internationals, while John Bumstead and Colin Pates were central to John Neal's exciting side in the 1980s, the blues brother Eddie Newton and Frank Sinclair big favourites in the 1990s, but the Chelsea youth were fading from the first team until only John Terry remained. It is no coincidence that he was the rock on which our most successful era was built.

None of this is to say that those brought in from other clubs can't become part of Chelsea in a similar way, with Frank Lampard an obvious example, but that has always been the case going back to the start via the likes of Zola, Dennis Wise, Kerry Dixon and so on. This is why the return of Frank as manager was extra-exciting and extra-special, an appointment that lifted so many people up. It really did feel like a fresh start, as if the supporters were finally getting part of their club back.

Frank returned in the same way that Eddie McCreadie and Roberto Di Matteo did, all three of them Chelsea to their core. Like Eddie before him, Frank started playing the youth, albeit it more modestly given the talent at his disposal. It is true that both had their hands forced, but at the same time they embraced the opportunity and it was fantastic to see. Again, like Eddie McCreadie, Frank Lampard's deep connection to the club has to be responsible for that readiness to play and develop the youngsters.

The current wave of young talent is probably the best since those Eddie Mac days, but nothing is ever easy, and just as Osgood and Hudson left in the early-1970s, and McCreadie in 1977, in recent years the axe has unfairly fallen on Di Matteo, Carlo Ancelotti and finally Frank, the big worry now that his departure will mean the end of the revolution. He had already seen big-money signings brought into the club with the end of the transfer ban, and while that may or may not have destabilised what he was trying to do, it couldn't have been good for the morale of those in the process of breaking through.

The good news so far is that Mason Mount and Reece James are established as Chelsea and England regulars, while Calum Hudson-Odoi is still in the frame, but then there are the sales of Tammy Abraham and Fikayo Tomori to Roma and Milan. Neither made much sense at the time, and seem like madness now, when we need a centre-forward who can score goals and a quality centre-half with those still at the club either ageing or looking for transfers. Abraham and Tomori remain England internationals and seem to have long futures ahead of them in the game. They should be developing those at Stamford Bridge. Just as Chelsea boy Declan Rice should be.

Billy Gilmour and Conor Gallagher are among the many young players out on loan, and the first of these has to be a worry given his appearances in the Chelsea first-team and the fact he is already a Scotland regular. He should be at Chelsea learning from N'Golo Kante, not wasting his time at Norwich. Likewise Gallagher, who has impressed during his previous loans and is doing the same at Crystal Palace, although Thomas Tuchel does seem interested in bringing him back.

Tuchel has given debuts to several young players this season, among them Harvey Vale and Lewis Hall, who have both impressed, but there have only been glimpses so far, and what happens next is probably more about the owner than the manager. Are those with the power and wealth going to keep spending huge sums on established stars who may or may not fit in, or do they draw on the talent already here, go with Chelsea fans eager to play for the club they love. In the end, it could well be decided by their own bond with the club, whether they understand and feel part of our history and culture, or if it is just about the business.

John King is the author of nine novels including 'The Football Factory', 'The Prison House' and 'Slaughterhouse Prayer. He co-owns London Books with Martin Knight and also promotes a monthly punk rock night, 'Human Punk', regularly hosted at iconic music venue the 100 Club on London's Oxford Street. For further information about John's work and to buy copies of his books visit www.london-books.co.uk

BEST DAYS OF OUR LIVES
Martin Knight

George Best was one of those rare footballers who transcended club loyalties. Such was his charisma, natural beauty, and cultural impact as our country's first pop star footballer, boys across the land adored, worshipped, and attempted to emulate him down the park and on the school pitch regardless of whether they supported Chelsea, Leeds, or Liverpool. And let's not forget the girls who swooned at the sight of his jet-black hair, cleft chin, and magnetic blue eyes. George was not only different class he was on a different plane altogether. Every club had its idols, but George was God floating nonchalantly above them all. Others who worshipped the guitar, not the ball, nominated Eric Clapton as the Almighty via paint-sprayed graffiti on urban walls but with GB it didn't need saying. He was. Amen.

I had an almost life-size pop art poster of him on my bedroom wall, Georgie in red on a clear white background, body swerving, a tuft of hair curling on his neck. He was the last thing I looked at most nights as I fell to sleep on the top bunk. At school some of the boys had brand new swanky George Best football boots. Up until then most of us wore heavy, clodhoppers, remnants of the Stanley Matthews era but these were sleek, more like loafers than boots, with laces positioned rebelliously on the side and the man's distinctive signature on every boot. Curiously the most talentless players among us seemed to bloom in these, instilling confidence where there was previously none. The same stardust didn't work quite as well with the green Peter Bonetti goalkeeper gloves, as I recall.

There was a persistent rumour in the 1970s that George was poised to join Chelsea. The same buzz travelled around Stamford Bridge a couple of decades later when it was said that Matt Le Tissier was going to sign any day now. We're still waiting. With George, Dave Sexton was going to apparently part with £300,000 for him at a time when the record transfer fee was the £225,000 Brian Clough's Derby County had forked out for the Leicester City defender David Nish. It sounded under-priced to me. It didn't happen. I find it hard to believe that a manager – Dave Sexton – who struggled to contain maverick talents like Peter Osgood and Alan Hudson would really want to take on a genius firebrand such as George. Alan and Peter both said in later years that George really wanted to come to Chelsea and I'm sure he did – but was he thinking the area rather than the club?

George *did* eventually come to Chelsea settling in a flat in Cheyne

Walk where fittingly other iconic creatives including Vera Brittain, Ralph Vaughan Williams, James Whistler and Mick Jagger had all lived at various times. But by now his creativity on the field was behind him. He was still an icon to many; his drinking and carousing the envy of the young men who had worshipped him as boys. He was doing what they aspired to except he was doing it in better looking bars and with better looking women. The press meanwhile painted a picture of a fallen idol propping up the bar of the nearby Phene Arms. The truth was somewhere in between.

George was an alcoholic, like his mother before him. Ann Best took her first drink at 44-years-of-age and was dead ten years later. During his heavy drinking years George still managed to sprinkle his wizardry far and wide: from Fulham to Fort Lauderdale, Dunstable to Detroit. He told me he felt that he played some of his best football for San Jose Earthquakes when he was in his 30s in the 1980s.

I met him in the early 2000s when I was offered the chance to write his book. I got the offer via his manager Phil Hughes; we had become friends when he moved to a house close to mine. The publisher summoned me and offered me a fixed fee. I asked for a share of the author royalty. The man on the other side of the desk picked up a phone and called his boss and said as if I wasn't there: 'I have the ghost here for the George Best book in front of me. He says he wants a royalty deal.'

Ghost? I knew I wasn't going to like what was about to be relayed to me.

'Look, Martin, we could get any old journo to write this. We are only offering this to you first because you live near George and have the best chance of pinning him down. Take it or leave it.'

Charming. I took it.

George was by now living in a converted dairy farm nestled in the Surrey countryside with only the dull hum of the M25 to remind that greater London was not very far away. He was living in idyllic circumstances I felt. Two much-loved ebullient red setters bounded around the garden and he and his young, pretty wife Alex seemed to me to be very much in love. They affectionately called one another "Bestie". He had just emerged from hospital with a new liver and was extremely frail. He was eating sparingly, and his armchair swallowed him up. I was lucky catching him at a time when he was reflective and unable to wander.

At this point in his life George had published at least three autobiographies. One by gossip columnist Ross Benson ('The Good, The Bad and The Bubbly'), another by his friend Michael Parkinson ('George Best: A Memoir') and most recently 'Blessed' with Roy Collins. The latter book characterised by its searing honesty was a thundering commercial success and our book 'Scoring At Half Time' was designed to ride the wave created by 'Blessed'. The title indicates what the publishers were looking for – this time they pushed George to dwell on the jocular, the risqué and the fun. 'Get something new,' they prompted me. I tried my best, but George was in a ponderous, thoughtful, and philosophical frame of mind. He didn't really want to talk about the high jinks, the birds, and the booze. And after what he had just been through, I don't blame him.

He was an absolute gentleman. Refusing to kiss and tell unless the person had kissed and told first. 'Check her book, not sure if she's ever gone public,' he'd say about various female sirens of the period. He also refused to be negative about any of his peers. 'I don't want anyone to read this book and feel upset by it.' He was full of love and praise. For Matt, for Denis, for Shay, and he even had kind words for Bobby Charlton who he had once had a frosty relationship with.

I went to the house one day and saw through the window that George was sitting down with his head in his hands. I didn't want to intrude on a private moment and felt embarrassed to knock on the door so tiptoed backwards and then made a bit of noise as I approached the door again, to alert him. Perhaps he had a headache or was he thinking I haven't got to do two hours with this bloke again, have I? I watched him gain strength on every visit and one day Alex answered the door and said he'd gone out in his Mini. I was put out that he'd done this when we had a meeting scheduled. Alex said try the bookies in Cheam. Sure enough that's where he was enveloped by working-class men in working-class clothes, banter, cigarette smoke, betting slips and stumpy pencils. He smiled broadly at me but made no excuse. How could I be cross? George was happy. He had taken his first step back to the pub.

The publishers booked a signing tour that was to encompass the main British cities. First up was Canary Wharf. The queues snaked around the block. George was nervous, sheepish almost. I think he thought the British public were unhappy with him over his cavalier relationship with his own health. No such worries. The fans piled in pouring out love for George and I watched him puff out and expand as each punter approached. At the end, and 200 books later, he said he had seen a coat on the Kings Road he wanted to buy, and he was going to catch a bus there. Despite protests from Phil, his manager, he disappeared into the throng. A late middle-aged man in dungarees and white tee shirt shimmying, feigning, and swerving through the office workers as only George Best could. I never saw him again.

He ended up holed up in a village pub surrounded by the prying cameras and the judgemental stormtroopers of the rolling news media. I then watched from a distance as George's life lurched towards its sad, depressing, and inevitable conclusion.

The media delighted in reporting his demise. Focusing on the negative, rarely the positive. I found the scrum outside the hospital unedifying. The invasion of a man's privacy in his dying days cruel and disrespectful. I don't think about those miserable times. I think of the boy from Belfast whose magnificent skills set the world alight and kidnapped the imagination of a generation. I remember how when very young I really believed he alone could take his small country of Northern Ireland to a World Cup Final. The Belfast boy. A boy who gave more pleasure than he ever took. Far, far more. A boy who didn't just live his wildest dreams, he lived ours too.

*Martin Knight's work has embraced many genres including true-crime, sport and fiction. He has collaborated with iconic footballers such as Peter Osgood, Charlie Cooke and George Best on their best-selling autobiographies and is a co-owner of London Books with John King. You can follow Martin on Twitter @MartinKnight_*

SATURDAY'S KIDS
Mark Meehan

You jump on the Number 52 bus to Victoria. You pile upstairs with your mates. Adult smoking is allowed only on the top deck of the bus. The air reeks of Benson & Hedges. A Quick game of bus pontoon. Your bus ticket had a four-digit number on its face and you added up the four numbers to see if it made 21. You jump off the bus (while it's still moving of course) at Notting Hill Gate and get the District Line train to Wimbledon.

Everyone jumps off at Fulham Broadway, you rush up the stairs with everyone all telling the hector you had got on the stop before at West Brompton and paying the difference in fare. Until barriers were introduced on London Underground, loss of revenue on match days across London football grounds suddenly took an upward turn. London Transport must have been skint every year especially when Chelsea were at home.

Into the Stamford Bridge cafe a few short steps away from Fulham Broadway station. While waiting for a free table you can gaze at the grainy black and white photographs of Chelsea players from a bygone era and the occasional colour photo featuring glory nights from Old Trafford and Athens. They were only a few years ago now but currently they feel like a lifetime away. A bygone era now as faded as some of the photos.

A cup of tea and a sausage sandwich and then that short walk to the ground. You had your first sight of the Stamford Bridge floodlights. That first feeling of anticipation. Chelsea at home. Saturday 3pm.

All around you the road to Stamford Bridge is full of traffic. The human kind. You pass the programme sellers, rosette sellers, roasted peanuts, hot dog and hamburger sellers on their mobile stalls. If you were not seduced by the mobile stall holders than there was always the quick detour to the club shop. CFC merchandise as varied as china football piggy banks, Bill Garner pennants and green, red and white scarves that paid homage to our Castrol GTX away kit. Happy days.

Onto the concourse, and the 'Goalden Goal' ticket seller tempts you every week to part with 50p to guess the time of the first goal of last goal. The continual "Get your 'Chelsea Goalden Goal' tickets" is part and parcel of every matchday but his loud air raid siren voice does get on your nerves very quickly. The first goal has a prize money of £50 the last goal £10 – what if it is 0-0 then is always the smart arse first time visitor question.

You get the same people every week going to the same seller. It is some kind of matchday superstition. It's not as is the sales pitch changed from one week to the next. Tickets are stuffed into wallets or coat pockets and long forgotten about.

You are stopped just before the turnstile entrance for the obligatory police search. Have you any offensive weapons on you today sir? Not today officer I need my oxyacetylene burner for the trip to Orient next week.

You buy the match day programme. I always put the programme in a plastic wallet and shove it up my jumper for safe keeping. I loved those 1970s Chelsea programmes – some say that football is art and if that is the case they were masterpieces like the football equivalent of a Constable or Rembrandt.

A tight squeeze at the turnstiles when a big game is on such as Palace or Spurs in the cup but you avoid the police horse trying to tap dance on your toes and you push through and with a click of the turnstiles you are in The Shed end.

Up the stairs into the Shed and having dodged the concourse sellers you run the gauntlet of White Wall Mick Tregent also flogging "get your lottery tickets, your Chelsea lottery tickets" at the top of the stairs. There was another seller who I think made a model of the East Stand out of match sticks or was it out of used losing lottery tickets? It was always good prize money. First prize £1000. Second Prize £500. Third Prize £100. But I never met or heard anyone who ever won any money.

Once you have climbed the concrete stairs you take your place on the right-hand side of The Shed. Not under cover but to the right near the floodlight pylons near the East Stand. From this vantage point you have a clear view of the action and your first view of the beautiful Stamford Bridge pitch.

Over the years you eventually move across to the White Wall, then to the middle of The Shed before eventually joining all the drinkers at the Tea Bar.

"We're all mad in the head, we're the Tea Bar not The Shed..."

Where ever you stood you felt at home and safe apart from the frequent invasions from the East London hordes. If anything you were probably more at risk from your own fans than any away fans. One time standing in the White Wall in the days of when smoking was allowed, and standing on the terraces it was not uncommon for the smell of slim panatelas or Benson & Hedges, a smell of burning revealed it was my jeans that were on fire due to a badly discarded cigarette. Thank heavens that flared trousers soon went out of fashion.

There was also the time I watched an FA Cup tie at home to Burnley standing ostrich-like on one foot for nearly 90 minutes as an early Paul Fletcher goal in the first minute for Burnley was equalised very quickly by a nimble Micky Droy beating the Burnley off side trap that sent everyone in the White Wall tumbling down the Shed terracing and with me losing my left shoe in the process. The remaining 85-minutes I observed my shoe gradually being thrown further and further down the terracing while Chelsea scored five more goals in the process. Celebrating a goal standing ostrich like on one foot is not to be recommended but it is the only thing you can do to avoid a ten-hole Dr Marten boot trampling on your uncovered toes every time there was surge forward.

Pre-match kick-off it was always DJ Pete Owen keeping the crowd entertained with all the top songs of the day, and he made the team changes announcement as a background accompaniment to everyone reading the programme cover-to-cover. Pete though was slow to catch up with the punk revolution of the late 70s especially as The Damned were first punk band to feature in the Chelsea programme. Back then there were no pyrotechnics or banner displays in The Shed, just Peter and his pre match spin to keep you entertained. Although I did worry when we played Birmingham City in 1979 and Pete put an advert in the programme for the following records to play on matchday: Long John Baldry, 'Let The Heartaches Begin'. Ken Dodd, 'Tears', and Elton John and Kiki Dee's, 'Don't Go Breaking My Heart.' We got relegated that year!

You could also guarantee in that one giant mass of people that there always be someone farting at Chelsea followed up by either a: "Wherever you be let your wind go free" or "Better out than in' and apologising for "the ruby I last night."

Then the moment when both teams come out on to the pitch from the bowels of the East Stand... emerging from a gap in the lower tier and The Shed would start singing:

"La la la la la la la la la la la Chelsea,
La la la la la la la la la la la Chelsea,
La la la la la la la la la la Chelsea,
La la la la la la la la la la Chelsea..."

The first-half ends, just as everyone is loitering on the stairs holding on to their half time piss in the hope that Chelsea might get a goal before the break.

You go for your half time of tea from Abraserve as everyone around you pisses up against the corrugated iron fence at the rear of The Shed and hope-against-hope that things in the second half would be better. You always miss the start of the second half as it takes an eternity for the staff to serve everyone. If you are feeling braver and hungry you go down the stairs beside the Tea Bar at the Bovril entrance for a half-time 'death burger' served with the immortal catch phrase, "Do you want onions with that?" I was never sure where the 'cook' washed his hands before serving the burgers and hot dogs.

The second-half would start and eventually a roar from The Shed would puncture the empty sky above SW6 when Chelsea would score to win an important game. And once more the end would sound like a

human radio as everyone would sing:
"And it's super Chelsea.
Super Chelsea FC,
We're by far the greatest team
The world has ever seen."

And on February 12, 2022, we were!

Mark Meehan is the founder of 'The Big Stamford Bridge Sleep Out' and former editor of the 'Chelsea Independent' fanzine which was published between 1987 and 2001. He is an active member of the Chelsea Supporters' Trust and has written and co-written a several books about The Blues. You can follow Mark on Twitter @eddiemacbawa

CHELSEA IN AMERICA
Beth Wild

We all have a slightly different story of how we found Chelsea. For me it was luck! I met a guy called Simon Turner at a party one Friday night that invited me to "a football match" the next day. Being in London for post-grad work and never seen a "soccer game", I thought why not. Little did I know how much it would change my life.

October 10, 1981
Football League Division Two
Chelsea 2 Wrexham 0
(Mike Fillery 59, Colin Lee 73)
Stamford Bridge
Attendance: 14,170
Referee: Mike Taylor

Chelsea: Petar Borota, Gary Locke, Chris Hutchings, Colin Viljoen, Colin Pates, Gary Chivers, Peter Rhoades-Brown, Ian Britton, Colin Lee, Alan Mayes, Mike Filery. (unused sub: Clive Walker) Manager: John Neal.

I fell in love with Chelsea, and the supporters that day. The atmosphere in The Shed and the singing and those lovely boys in Blue, especially Clive Walker. It was heaven really. I made a lifelong friend in Simon, one of the best friends in my life.

I learned a lot that season, not just how the game was played, the songs and all about Chelsea. I learned what it meant to be a Chelsea supporter. Going home and away no matter how cold, rainy or how far. That you always supported the team, "win or lose up the Blues". After all we were in Division Two, but for me we were "the greatest team the world had ever seen". But what Simon made perfectly clear was that this passion was actually a bit of missionary work. Every person he met, the first things he would ask, "Who do you support?" unless the answer was a fervent Chelsea, he made it his mission to explain to them why they were missing the essence of life, being a Chelsea supporter. He just could not fathom why anyone would not be a Chelsea supporter. I had never seen such passion. How could anyone not want to be on the Fulham Road every other Saturday and cheering on those wonderful Blue Boys?

When I left to go home to the United States of America, Simon told me, "Find more Chelsea supporters, create more Chelsea supporters".

1982 in the US was a football desert, I struggled to find anyone that even knew the game. But I tried, my youngest brother, Rob, being the first.

Through those dark times I would go back to Chelsea from time-to-time. Simon and I would go to a match and I would absorb all I could while I was there. At home I discovered ways of following, driving 45 minutes to get the Sunday London papers on Wednesday. Around 1990 I was over for a visit and Simon really showed his belief and passion. We were at a match and in a lull he turned to me to say, "you know one day Chelsea are going to be massive, they will be huge in America, and you will be a part of the biggest supporters club". Understand that in 1990 I still had not met ONE Chelsea supporter in the USA. I just laughed and told him he was high. But he refused to accept that, "It will happen, just be ready, don't give up!"

Fast-forward to 1996 and my first internet connection, the first website I looked for was Chelsea's, thank god for Jax. It was wonderful, that fire started to grow, I had to find others. A few years later I was in Washington DC and one of the first 'live' televised games. My poor brother, John was tasked with finding a place to watch the match. He was dogged, but found a place called Summers in Arlington. It looked like a Denny's, but in the back there was a bar, and to my utter joy and astonishment, it was FULL OF CHELSEA SUPPORTERS!!! I had found my home in the US. Tim Bird welcomed me to the DC Blues, and what an experience. From there the fire was roaring. I ended up meeting so many, an underground network of fabulous supporters, Nick 'Tuna' Jordan, Mike and Steve Neat, Chris 'Wobbley' Bowley, Harris 'Chopper' Reife and more. Trips to New York and DC ensued and the first trip to the Bridge with my new friends. Simon was grinning from ear to ear, he was certain the takeover had started.

Then the summer tour of 2004. Chelsea came to America, and I was over the moon. Plans made, and we were all so excited. Thanks to Steven Cohen and his Football show it was easier to get the word out as to where we would meet up in Seattle. That weekend will be forever etched in my mind. Not just for meeting John Terry for the first time. It was being with maybe 100 Chelsea supporters from around the country and the UK. More importantly meeting Andy Burbidge, little did I know what a friend he would become. Andy and I are shared souls, and his passion and need to find and make Chelsea supporters was just like Simon's. Through three matches that summer our friendship solidified. It wasn't the Bridge but it was so fantastic, and I couldn't help but call Simon to tell him his dream had started.

Shortly after the tour ended, Andy called one morning to see if I could get on the internet. He directed me to www.tx_blues.com and there in front of my eyes, on my birthday was a website with a photo of me and JT and the statement, "ARE YOU CHELSEA? ARE YOU IN TEXAS? THINK YOU ARE ALONE, YOU ARE NOT", and then my email. I was overjoyed and instantly called Simon to share the link and he was so happy, and all he could say was, "See I told you!"

Believe it or not people found me and by the end of the season we had a band of 36 of us spread across Texas, JR Root, Cary Eddy, John Bruzda, Jens and others. We stayed in touch, we made plans for our first trip, and were allowed to form an official supporters club by Chelsea. We won the (Premier) League that year, the first time in 50 years, and it was crazy. I wasn't there at the Bridge, but with friends and our growing supporters club in Texas. We were still meeting in member's homes, but it was a moment I will never forget. Standing next to Steve as he fell to his knees in tears. The phone ringing off the hook with calls from Blues around the country, the utter elation. Then to Simon, to share that day with him as best I could.

Another tour that summer and the word was getting out, Wrayman (Andy Wray) from So Cal, Paul Peltz from Tennessee and so many others. That was when Andy and I envisioned a network of local supporters' clubs that would work together to spread the word about Chelsea. To create a following here in the US, that would grow and become CIA, Chelsea in America.

Andy Burbidge and I kept spreading the word and taking every opportunity to invite people in, to give them a place to be, a place to make friends and get up at stupid-thirty in the morning and drive to a pub in the dark and watch the mighty Blues battle on. To spread our history, our traditions, and what it really means to be Chelsea. That idea of sharing and educating all that it means to be Chelsea is still one of the most important parts of a Supporters Club. Chelsea is a London club, graced with the finest group of supporters in the land, with a great history and a wonderful set of traditions that we are happy to adopt, learn and continue.

Making trips to the Bridge with those that were going for the first time, has gifted me with many memories. The wild-eyed wonder and thrill of the initiate and the amazing camaraderie of those that go every week. They continue this tradition of "breaking in" first timers. They are as intricate to the growth in America as any of us here. I (we) owe so much to them, Chris Axon, CFC Cathy (Catherine McDonnell), DJ (David Johnstone), Marco (Mark Worrall), Spy (Neil Barnett), Mark Coden, Steve and Daz (the Mantle twins), Rick Glanvill, Chidge (David Chidgey) and everyone at the Chelsea Fancast, Mark 'Elvis' Goddard and Ledge at the Museum, Cazza (Caroline Rice), Frances (Clarke) and Lizzi (Durham), and so many others I cannot name them all.

As CIA grew, unfortunately Simon became seriously ill and tragically passed away before he could see his beloved Blues hoist that trophy with the big ears. But I know he was watching. I heard him on that day, whispering in my ear, "We got this" before Drogs kicked that ball and we all went mental. He was on my shoulder and saying, "See I told you" as I was crammed in a pub in Dallas (thanks BJ) in a shower of beer. The Army continues to grow, and though I stepped down from leading the

CIA a couple of years ago. What fabulous hands our future is in, thanks to John Costello, Allison Kasic, Brian Woolf and quite a few others, they now carry that flame, and it is growing and getting brighter.

In the end that missionary work of spreading the word, paying it forward, is what has given me a lifetime of memories that would take a book to fill. It is about sharing and being that voice of support for Chelsea, and it is about "the greatest supporters in the world". Thank you to all for making my life amazing, for helping me to take what Simon gave me and pay it forward.

Chelsea missionary Beth Wild continues to spread the True Blue word whenever and wherever the opportunity presents itself. Her work will never be done. You can find Beth on Twitter @TX_Blue

YOUR CHELSEA MASCOT IS...
Chris Wright

From my very first visit to Stamford Bridge in the 1989/90 season I never looked back and was always anticipating my next match. My earliest memories were standing in 'The Shed' with my Dad and older brothers and we'd bring a little foot stool in with us so I could see. The guys on the turnstiles would often let us in for free as they did for many children in those days. Win, lose or draw it didn't really bother me. The atmosphere, the programme, the smell of hotdogs and onions and don't get me wrong, if Kerry Dixon popped up with a winner it was extra special.

Glenn Hoddle's arrival at Stamford Bridge as our new player manager was a huge boost in the summer of 1993. With Ian Porterfield being sacked midway through the 1992/93 season and ex-blue David Webb taking charge for the rest of that season a big appointment was due with the club needing a new direction. Glenn had just won promotion to the Premier League with Swindon Town via the play-offs as player manager and it was now a perfect opportunity for him to take the step up with Chelsea.

Glenn stated in his programme notes for his opening game as Blues boss against Blackburn Rovers (August 14, 1993); "My aim is to be as successful as I possibly can. The club has not had much success recently and I will be trying to help us win some silverware. But it is important how we get success. I wouldn't want to get it by playing dreadful football. The principle of winning by playing good football means a great deal to me".

Hoddle's first signing as Chelsea manager was a notable one, Gavin Peacock. £1.25 million secured his services from Newcastle United and he was a very exciting prospect having made a big impact in the North-East. Peacock could play either as an attacking midfielder or striker and after scoring the opener on his debut against Rovers he quickly became a favourite with supporters. Unfortunately, the game saw the visitors turn things around to win 2-1!

Despite this defeat, the football was much better to watch with Hoddle implementing his own style and not long after his reign as Chelsea player-manager began something quite extraordinary happened to me... I was 10-years-4-months-and-15 days-old.

Saturday September 25, 1993
Premier League
Chelsea 1-0 Liverpool

TALES FROM THE SHED

(Neil Shipperley 48)
Stamford Bridge
Attendance: 31,271
Referee: Keith Hackett

Chelsea: Dimitri Kharine, Frank Sinclair, Mal Donaghy (Gareth Hall 58), Andy Dow, Steve Clarke, Jacob Kjeldbjerg, Eddie Newton, Glenn Hoddle, Dennis Wise, Tony Cascarino, Neil Shipperley. (unused subs: Kevin Hitchcock, John Spencer) Manager: Glenn Hoddle.

Up until this game I had only watched Chelsea a handful of times and unfortunately without great success! It must have been around mid-September when my Dad asked me a question to which there was only ever going to be one answer. "Do you fancy going to the Chelsea v Liverpool game in a couple of weeks?" Immediately I was buzzing and replied with an emphatic "YES!!!" He said, "That's good, but there's one other thing." "What's that then?" I asked. "Would you like to be the mascot for the day?' I couldn't believe what he had just said to me. I was overjoyed that I was about to meet all my Chelsea heroes and lead the team out onto the pitch with Dennis Wise!!!!!! We had three tickets in the Director's Box and the day would be shared with obviously my Dad and my eldest brother Steve.

Despite all of Chelsea's success in recent years which I feel very privileged to have been part of, this day remains my greatest day as a Chelsea supporter. I remember soon after being told about this I attempted to sell my Gameboy in order to raise some money to be spent in the club shop on the day. A 'for sale' note soon went up in the window of our local corner shop and I managed to get £40 for it! On the day itself I was excited and quite nervous at the same time. Playing Liverpool was never going to be easy and a win would just top off a perfect day.

We went for an early pizza down the Fulham Road before heading to the club shop to buy souvenirs to get signed. We quickly made our way to the main reception where I was greeted with a programme (which I was in) and a replica home kit. I was excited! Once I was changed and into my kit we headed to the dressing room to meet the players. Before we went in we had a quick chat with Glenn Hoddle and Peter Shreeves who were in an adjacent room clearly talking tactics. Glenn then asked me if I was going to bring the team luck today. I obviously replied 'yes'. As we walked into the dressing room it appeared very relaxed and good humoured. My Dad actually brought along his video camera and we have some great footage, with John Spencer mainly being the joker among the pack. We met all the players and got photos as well as signed footballs and autographs. When meeting Dennis Wise my brother Steve (14 at the time) came out with an absolute classic, "You playing today Dennis?" His reply was, "I hope so." Wisey was obviously club captain.

Once we had met all the players it was time for me to take to the famous Stamford Bridge pitch where I had a kick about with the one and only Stamford The Lion. I scored a few penalties against him in front of a few fans who had chosen to get a good spot in The Shed as supposed to being in the pub. From the age of ten I could always say that I scored at Stamford Bridge. As I finished scoring goals past Stamford I joined the players warming up and I remember kicking the ball around with Dennis Wise and Andy Dow. Shaking hands with Dmitri Kharine before returning to the changing rooms praying he would keep a clean sheet. As the players made their final preparations I was asked to wait in the tunnel for Dennis Wise to meet me. I then led the team out in front of 30,000-plus Chelsea fans, a packed Stamford Bridge with The Shed belting out 'Glenn Hoddle's blue and white army'.

As the referee met with the captains (Dennis Wise and Ian Rush) my Dad was still on the pitch with his video camera (he wasn't allowed to). Once the coin had been tossed to decide who was shooting which way in the first-half we lined up and at that point I think the officials and players thought my dad was Chelsea's official photographer who we later realised didn't turn up to work. The officials quickly made it clear to my dad that he needed to get off the pitch quickly as they had a game to start! The referee gave me the 10p piece that he had made the toss with and I jogged off the pitch. My Dad and brother Steve were by the tunnel and we were quickly taken up to our seats in the East Stand Director's Box.

What I actually remember from the game itself is very little as there was so much going on throughout the day. Looking back at footage of the match I was reminded that we were very fortunate and Liverpool had many chances and probably should have won the game. Fortunately for me it was Chelsea who won the match 1-0 with an early second-half strike from Neil Shipperley. The referee confirmed that the ball had crossed the line after a fumble by Liverpool goalkeeper Bruce Grobbelaar. We hung on for the win but at the time it was a massive three points for us. Typically, after this impressive victory, Chelsea didn't win another league match until December 28! Why was it that we could beat the big teams but then struggle against sides we were expected to roll over? This was definitely a Blues trait that lasted many years… and still happens occasionally today even though since 1993 the Club has enjoyed phenomenal success.

After the game I got to meet the goal scorer Neil Shipperley and chairman Ken Bates. What an incredible day and a very unique experience. Thank you Dad!

A Chelsea season ticket holder and writer for the 'cfcuk' fanzine, Chris Wright's first book 'Blue Days: The transformation of Chelsea under Hoddle, Gullit and Vialli' was published in 2020. You can follow him on Twitter @chriswrightzz

BEST FOOTBALL FRIEND
Rick Glanvill

Inter-club rivalry is the warp and weft of football, the fundamental of its fabric. Without jeopardy there is no sport. Strip the game of schadenfreude and you create a disturbance in The Force. But overstep the mark and you jeopardise a lifelong friendship. Bragging rights are for acquaintances and colleagues. Proper fans perform a post-match dance as elaborate as medieval courtly love.

I've danced that match day madrigal with plenty of mates over the decades, sticking to the unspoken rules no matter what happened on the pitch, however high or low the outcome. And the challenge to remain cordial after the final whistle is never tougher than when one of your greatest friends is a fervent Liverpudlian.

Barney and I go way back and our lives have intertwined like ivy: music, mischief, laughs, politics – we've even pooled our football delight when United or Arsenal took a smashing. We met at Newcastle. He was the first student to show me how to cry in front of the tutor to secure a deadline extension and was a heat-sync for incident. When I started a successful reggae, Latin, funk music night in the Toon in 1983 Barney was a doorman next to the club bouncer Hetty, a trans-gangster in an XXXL nightie. He started a band, The Shed, that was hailed on BBC Radio 4 as the world's worst.

After we left the North-East our families spent dozens of mini-breaks together; our wives and sons are great friends too. We've both long been home and away supporters and have a yesterglow of memories communicated in every medium from postcard to WhatsApp.

The first time we actually went to a Liverpool-Chelsea game together was in May 1985, a preposterous 4-3 setback for John Neal's renaissance men. I stayed at Barney's then singleton flat and mentioned never going to Anfield before. He pulled out a VHS of their golden years and left it on while cooking breakfast. It was tough not to grimace 'make it stop' but I found something genial to say. We moved on to stadiums in general and agreed any ground where players entered the arena from a corner was rank. We didn't know Hillsborough was about to change all that forever.

February 1992 was the high spot of Ian Porterfield's spell as manager. We stayed at Barney's house in Warrington had a raucous Friday night out including Mr Smith's nightclub in an ironic homage to Michaela Strachan and 'Hitman And Her', which was filmed there. The assassins the next day, though, were ex-Wimbledonians Dennis Wise (who also missed a penalty) and Vinnie Jones. The evening paper was scandalised, splashing: 'Reds Mugged By Crazy Gang'. That was Chelsea's first win at Anfield since 1935 and Liverpudlian noses were out of joint in the debrief at the nearby George.

"Come on, you can at least congratulate us for one league win in 57 ******* years."

"Draw would've been fair. Macca had to score near the end."

We entered the age of texting in 1994 and that November I took the afternoon off with a Chelsea mate and trained it up for the match. Barney met me at Bank Quay. It was someone's birthday and from 4.30 to kick-off and the road to the game was paved with bad intentions. I recall a Country and Western bar, not enough tapas in a Latino joint, and a brief duck-in at the closest pub to the ground, the Albert. We rolled into the away end like sailors, the plimsoll line of pints long submerged. The game was an unprecedented blur. Sitting in the nearby George afterwards we at least figured out we'd taken the lead but then lost 3-1. Barney came bounding in.

"Thought you'd do us again! What did you make of the sending-off?"

"What sending-off?!" We hadn't even registered Erland Johnsen's marching orders. Never been drunk at a game since.

It was fascinating to see the progressive mothballing of the area: whole streets of dense, attractive Victorian houses surrounding the ground sparsely occupied, then virtually empty, and finally boarded up. Even the dog sh*t disappeared from the streets.

The VHS having failed its brainwashing a decade earlier, Barney invited me to sample the Kop itself for the Blues' final visit before its demolition in 1994.

The air of stalled regeneration spawned opportunism that is unlikely to happen at any other ground, such as 'Our Arthur's' on Anfield Road. Once one of many huge mid-Victorian villas, Arthur's was an illegal bar occupying the basement of what seemed like a care home.

Those who'd booked matchday parking in its grounds had their name scrawled on a paper plate staked in the flower bed. Barney once claimed I was the first opposition fan ever sneaked inside. Looking at the exposed electrical wiring, low ceiling and clutter, I wondered how much of a privilege that would be in event of a fire.

It was a bar that had jumped out of bed and thrown anything on to answer the door. Nothing matched. A clutter of pub ephemera, leftovers from successive trends, battled with more scrappily obsessive ephemera than a stalker's porn dungeon. The barman just laughed when I offered to a bit of Blues memorabilia to complement the Red shrine. No history, see. Nor a proper adversary.

Like a grubby TV studio that scrubs up for the cameras, the Spion Kop sanctum was as decrepit as the old Shed or West Stand and boasted as many quiet, taking-it-in tourists as hoary-handed Scousers au fait with the second verse of 'Fields of Anfield Road.' There was no mystique but I was glad to have gone.

We were down and out inside 20 minutes that day, and matches up there in the late 1990s went pretty much the same way. The balance shifted dramatically over 98 dazzling days in 2003, starting with the 2-1 win against the Merseysiders at the Bridge. Financial strife averted, Champions League football secured, Roman Abramovich arrived in July as a gale of fresh air and a force of nature.

People forget that two months later the first league game of the Roman era was a 2-1 victory at Liverpool. I didn't text 'ships passing in the night' after that but I recognised the motion. Later that same season, March 2004, I was in the North-West on business and saw the Reds had a UEFA Cup match against Marseille. Barney rustled a ticket and I went. At half-time, in a different stand and lacking a programme to check for myself, I texted him:

"Who's that amazing striker upfront for Marseille?!"
"DROBGA or something. Handful."
"Absolutely running it. Want him at Chelsea."

Early the following season under Mourinho it was obvious we were genuine title favourites for the first time in my lifetime. Barney was genuinely excited when I asked, "You've been there loads of times in the past. How d'you know when your team is good enough?" I kind of knew, but wanted to give him an investment in the moment.

"You think you've experienced it before but you haven't. It's a different sensation. You always have the answers. You're that much better than other teams. Shots that could stray wide go in. Decisions go your way. There's an air of inevitability."

That novel sensation was overwhelming when New Year's Eve was spent with our families watching whizzbangs outside Paddy's Wigwam, then Joe Cole scored the only goal the following day. So that when we met in the Champions League a few days after Frank Lampard's goals secured the title at Bolton, I occupied the loftier ground in our football relationship for the first time in 30 years.

There was deference before the game and, after Luis Garcia's 'ghost goal' secured victory, I detected the kind of punching-upwards ebullience I'd felt after those shock wins against the European champions in 1978, '81 and even '92. I spent the aftermath parrying jibes in The Granton, inoculated by the title win and opiated by consolation drinks. My Chels compadre Kass traded his pre-booked hotel and flights for Istanbul to Barney's pal Paul. It remains Barney's greatest night in a football ground.

Suddenly, vital and controversial cup clashes with Liverpool followed with unprecedented regularity, requiring diplomacy; a Cold War detente approach to banter. No proper fan carps about a victory to a supporter of the defeated who's also a friend. Especially when it matters so much. Instead: radio silence before and courteous observations afterwards.

"Things might've been different had Čech not saved that from Carroll."

"City still have to win their games in hand to beat you to the title."

Another brief moment of openness came in 2012 when we reached the Champions League final. I asked Barney what feelings to expect if we won it. (They'd won it five times, you know.)

"Ecstasy for a week. A daily tingle for a month or two. Constant pick-me-up for a year. Then you relive it all on the anniversary." He was absolutely spot on.

The intensity has passed now. We duet on WhatsApp, slagging off United or the Arse, and meet up as football equals. I even congratulated my great mate on their first title win in 30 years. But of course I didn't really mean it.

Rick Glanvill is Chelsea FCs official historian and has written for the Club's official publications and website since 1993. Rick collaborated with Chelsea legend Paul Canoville on his best-selling autobiography 'Black and Blue' which won 'Best Autobiography' at the 2009 'British Sports Books Awards. Follow him on Twitter @RickGlanvill

CHELSEA'S DEBT TO JOHN NEAL
Gary Thacker

Chelsea are currently one of the top clubs in Europe. Champions League trophies, Premier League titles and domestic cups jostle for position in a trophy cabinet full of glittering silverware, thanks to a roster of world-class players, guided by some of the game's most celebrated coaches. That wasn't always the case though. Blues fans of my age will easily recall the days, forty years ago, when thoughts of the club being European champions were the stuff of outlandish dreams. Languishing in Division Two the need wasn't for a superstar manager, but for one who understood the less exalted strata of English football, someone who could identify talent available at reasonable prices, and knew how to build a successful team. Fortunately, the club decided that John Neal was the man for the job. There really couldn't have been a better fit.

In his four years at Stamford Bridge, before ill health demanded a premature retirement from the game, he achieved promotion back to the top tier, produced a vibrant team, delivered a rare period of stability and progressed the squad with a number of astute signings. Whilst many more famous mangers will rightly be included in a list of the most important people to have taken charge at Chelsea; Mourinho, Ancelotti, Di Matteo, Conte and Tuchel come to mind, any such roll of honour would be incomplete should the name of John Neal not be lauded amongst them.

As was the case with so many players, and managers, of that era, Neal was a child of the industrial North-East, born into the mining community of Seaham, County Durham. Indeed, his first club was Silkworth Colliery, where he played as a teenage full-back when the country was recovering from the privations and tragedies of the World War Two. In the spirit of the area, he was an uncompromising defender, vigorous in the tackle, but also blessed with the game intelligence to become a skilled footballer. Hull City took him into the full-time professional game of league football in 1949. Although he'd stay on Humberside for five seasons, they were difficult times, and Neal struggled to make any meaningful impact at the club. In 1956, he moved to Kings Lynn. It was the sort of step down to lower grade football that insistently informs any young aspiring footballer that it's time to abandon dreams of fame and fortune in the game. Neal was, however, made of sterner stuff.

Perhaps it was the Norfolk air. Perhaps it was that Hill City had failed to spot the nascent talent he had. More likely, however, it was Neal's dogged determination to succeed that turned his time with Kings Lynn from the first step on a downward spiral, into the launching pad for his return to the league football. In July 1957, he had impressed sufficiently for Swindon Town to take him back to the full-time game. The road now resolutely pointed upwards.

In 1959, after becoming a key element of the Swindon defence, and captain of the club, Aston Villa manager Joe Mercer saw him as the ideal player to help the recently relegated Birmingham club back into the top division, and took him to Villa Park. In his first season with the club, Villa won the Division Two title, and then followed up by lifting the inaugural League Cup the following season. Whilst other players may have been the stars of the team, the unassuming, experienced Neal was every bit as important to the success of the club, providing calming influence and bedrock of the defence. Success had come late in Neal's career and, now into his thirties, Villa decided that he should be moved on in 1962. A move to Southend United looked like another herald of a career being wound down. In typical Neal fashion however, he would turn this supposed decline in fortunes into another launching pad.

At Southend, Neal played under manager Alvan Williams. The experienced and astute Welshman had identified him not only as the sort of experienced player who could serve the club well on the pitch, but also as someone who would develop into a coach as well. The move fitted Neal like a hand in a glove. The following year, Williams was persuaded to return to Wales and take over at Wrexham. Taking Neal with him as an assistant was an obvious move, and there was plenty of forward planning involved.

Williams would retire at the end of the season and, by that time, Neal's experience of working under him was considered sufficient for him to be given the manager's job. The cub would reap huge dividends from Williams's foresight. In nine seasons at the Racecourse Ground, Neal would not only identify and develop a string of talented players such as Mickey Thomas and Joey Jones, both who went on to play at the highest levels of the game and would enjoy seasons at Stamford Bridge, but also delivered unheralded success. Success in the Welsh Cup led to undreamt of exploits in European competition, on one occasion progressing to the quarter-finals of the European Cup Winners Cup, until losing out to eventual tournament winners Anderlecht by a single goal. Domestically, as well as promotion charges, hugely profitable cup runs not only swelled the club's coffers, but also saw triumphs over the likes of Spurs and Sunderland.

Much as Villa had snapped up Neal from lower league Swindon Town, after Jack Charlton left Middlesbrough, and the team's stars were sold off, the Ayresome Park club's hierarchy took Neal back to his native North-East hoping he could perform similar magic there. Despite the Boro fans voicing dissent over the appointment of a relatively low-profile manager, Neal's adherence to attacking football quickly won the doubters over, as he established the club in Division One. In 1981 however, when the proposed sale of Craig Johnston to Liverpool looked likely to be the start of another financially driven sell-off, tearing apart the young progressive team he had created, Neal refused to sit by and watch his work being dismantled. He left the club.

Boro's loss was Chelsea's gain. The following season, with Neal at Stamford Bridge, Middlesbrough finished bottom of the league and were relegated. The money received for Johnston looked like scant compensation for losing both their top division status and the manager who had picked up the club and driven it forward. At the end of the previous season, Boro had finished mid-table in the top tier, with Chelsea in a similar position in the division below.

Ken Bates had bought Chelsea for the princely sum of £1, and was looking for an answer to the club's travails both on and off the pitch. A series of crossed-fingers, quick-fix solutions of employing celebrated names such as Geoff Hurst and Danny Blanchflower to the managerial role, had been mixed in with the more sedate times of Ken Shellito and former club full-back Eddie McCreadie. The Scot had gained promotion for the club, before a reported bust-up over a club car had seen the former Shed favourite walk away. Back down in the second tier, with instability and repeated crises on the pitch, it hardly looked like an enticing prospect for any manager. Fortunately for Chelsea, John Neal wasn't just 'any manager'.

Any club in that sort of predicament takes some time to turn around though and Neal's first season at Stamford Bridge was preoccupied by a fight against a potentially disastrous relegation to Division Three. A paltry 11 wins all season shouted of crisis but, with the new manager's influence gradually hauling the club back from the brink, turning losses into draws and draws into priceless wins. A two-point gap was sufficient for salvation. Neal now had time to begin work on pointing things in the right direction.

Reshaping his squad and employing more progressive tactics, the Neal revolution got under way, and even persuaded the irascible Bates to trust his judgment and invest in some new players – many of whom would become legends at the club. The owner was originally aghast at the cost of bringing in a young striker from Reading. The sum of £150,000 was bad enough, but a further £25,000 should the player achieve international honours was deemed both excessive, but also unlikely to occur. Years later, that money would seem like a bargain when stacked against the return that Kerry Dixon delivered. His partnership with David Speedie would excite all Blues fans of the era, and exasperate those of our opponents.

Many other Neal acquisitions became outstanding successes at the club, and also proved to be sound investments. Pat Nevin was signed from £95,000 from Clyde and, after five years of impish play and crowd-pleasing wing play, was sold to Everton for more than double that amount. Influential midfielder Nigel Spackman, at £35,000 looked a bargain. Four years later, that figure looked more like robbery as Chelsea received £400,000 from Liverpool for his signature. Chelsea paid Morton £100,000 for Joe McLaughlin, who offered stalwart defensive service for half-a-dozen years before moving to Charlton Athletic for £650,000. Neal also dipped back into his time at Wrexham to sign the ever-popular goalkeeper Eddie Niedzwiecki, who had been a youngster with the North Wales club when Neal was there.

This was no buy low, sell high policy though. The profits made on players were an adjunct to the success on the field. Just a single season after that relegation scare, Neal's magic had made Chelsea Division Two champions and we marched proudly back into the top tier of the English game. In a 42-game season, Chelsea had seen their colours lowered on a mere four occasions, with his attacking team scoring 90 goals on their way to dominating the division. In contrast, Middlesbrough only just escaped relegation, finishing in seventeenth position. The fortunes of Chelsea and Middlesbrough were like those weather charms where, when the sun shines one is out, and the other is hidden inside, with the situation reversed when it rains. Chelsea were enjoying some sunlit days, with clouds casting doom over Middlesbrough. The man dictating the weather was John Neal.

Whilst as a club, Chelsea have a history of creating internal difficulties for themselves, at other times fate has dealt a cruel hand. In 1984, with all the prospects appearing positive, just 52 at the time, Neal was taken seriously ill and required heart surgery. He recovered, with Chelsea achieving an outstandingly impressive sixth place finish, but it was an ill portent of things to come. His club was in the rudest of health, but the man who head breathed new life into Chelsea was seriously ill. After that single season in the top flight with Chelsea's future looking set for success, Neal was compelled to hand over the reins of the club to John Hollins.

Understandably keen to retain Neal's influence at the club, Chelsea offered their ailing former manager a position as director of the club. Wanting to keep an eye on the success of the team he had built, Neal accepted, but even that role would not be tenable for long. Further surgery, and retirement from the club followed in 1986. Although still honoured by the club, Neal was now merely a fan. Along with fans such as myself, he watched as the club moved on, and would have rejoiced in the Abramovich years with long overdue silverware arriving. Fate spared him to see the club's greatest moment, as Drogba's penalty made his club, the one he had picked up and put back on track, Champions of Europe. It must have made him wonderfully happy. Two years later, in November 2014, despite his dogged determination to fight, John Neal's heart finally gave in and he passed away, aged 82.

The length of times that I've been a Chelsea means that I've seen many ups and downs and remember, with a smile, the days when John

Neal arrived as Chelsea's saviour and his young thrusting team launched into the top tier and laid about them with the vigour of youth, opportunity and conviction, as Dixon, Speedie and Nevin wreaked havoc with the supposed top teams. Such joy however is also tinged with regret at what might have been, but never came to fruition. Neal's time at the top of the game, was short, but so very sweet at Stamford Bridge. Even with the success the club is now enjoying, I still remember the joy, hope and success that John Neal brought to Chelsea. He should always be lauded for those days. We owe him that.

Gary Thacker has published a number of football books and regularly writes for select magazines and websites. His latest book 'Out Of The Blue: Chelsea's Unlikely Champions League triumph' is out now. Find out more on Twitter @ootb2012

WORK EXPERIENCE
Chelsea Chadder

Many years ago, when I was just 15-years-old, my school friends and I had to do a week-and-a-half of 'vocational experience' as part of our schoolwork. The idea was to gain some valuable experience in the workplace in order to get a taste of things to come. We could either let the school arrange our placement, or we could organise it ourselves. Some of my friends went to a local vet, newspaper or their dad's workplace. However, this wasn't my sort of thing. When I was 15 I was only interested in one type of career; professional football!

I grew up living on the Sussex coast, and so the easiest option would be to contact Brighton & Hove Albion Football Club. Although I love football, BHAFC is not my team. The team I support is Chelsea! Therefore, with my Dad's help, I contacted Chelsea Football in the Community (FITC) to ask if I could help out there. They were more than happy for me to come in and see how the FITC team works. Sadly, my school said that the 120-mile round trip would be too far to travel each day. Too far for who?! Basically, a teacher was meant to come and observe me in my workplace and they weren't prepared to do that.

After some negotiations it was decided I could go. I was over the moon. I mean, getting the train to Stamford Bridge everyday was hardly a chore! The only downside was the timing of the work experience. I had to do eight days work in July, so none of the players, etc, were likely to be around. I didn't mind; I got to wear a Chelsea shirt to work every day and be around the football club I loved.

On my first day I remember turning up and being asked to make loads of cups of tea and coffee. Pretty standard stuff. Another job I had to do was inflate footballs in the storeroom, which was full of all kinds of Chelsea goodies. It was great to have a little sneak around. I remember finding a load of old Chelsea scratch cards with Glenn Hoddle on the front. They were out of date so I scratched a load off. All I can say is that the club must have made a fortune from this as hardly any of them had any winners!

Anyway, I had two main jobs to do each day. The first was to prepare party food for children's parties that took place in the Stamford Bridge Press Room. I was given a large set of keys and was allowed to let myself into the tunnel entrance, just next to the East Stand reception. I went on a tour of Stamford Bridge recently and how things have changed! I used to go into the spare changing room and make jam sandwiches, plate up biscuits and crisps, etc, and then set up the press room for the party. Perhaps one of the most fulfilling jobs in my life! Being left alone to work in a Chelsea changing room. Brilliant!!! I could see the old baths, tactics board, but sadly no player shirts.

Another great job was to help with the tours of Stamford Bridge with one of the other FITC staff members. The tour was much different then, especially as it's only the East Stand that is still standing! I was like a sponge on the first day, soaking up all the information. It was so fascinating.

After the eight days of a great experience I had to return to school for the last two days of the week and write a presentation on the experience. My presentation involved a prop, which I will tell you about now.

Although I had to return to school for the last two days, I decided that it would be more beneficial to spend the last day back at Chelsea! I took the train as normal and made my way to Stamford Bridge. I made the teas and coffees and was then told that Ruud Gullit may be at the Bridge later. I was so excited by the prospect of meeting him! The FITC office was across the road from the ground and didn't have a fax machine. Therefore, a FITC staff member and I had to go to the East Stand, and head to the second floor to send the fax and pick up the post. I took one of my Chelsea shirts with me and left it with the receptionist to ask Ruud if he would sign it when he comes in.

Later that day I had to set up a birthday party. It was quite a big one and there was loads of rubbish. I searched around to find a bin to put it in but there were none around. I went outside and headed back down the side of the East Stand saw the then Chairman of Chelsea, Ken Bates. He called me over and asked what I was doing! A little nervous and in awe I just said I was looking for a bin to put this rubbish in. His reply was to throw it over the fence and let it be British Rail's problem. He was, of course, joking and said carry on. Phew!

After the party was set up I had to get the midday post from the East Stand second floor. On the way down the lift stopped on the first floor. Who walked in? The new Chelsea Manager, Ruud Gullit. He was huge, and I was completely overwhelmed. However, I quickly picked up the courage to ask him if he would sign my shirt. He was more than happy to. Imagine that, a Chelsea mad 15-year-old meeting a European and World Player of the Year, and now the new manager of Chelsea at Stamford Bridge!

My heart was racing and my mind was thinking a million thoughts, especially as my dad was coming to meet me a few hours later! I still had to help with a tour of the ground that afternoon. When I got back to the office there was a bit of a panic. The guy who did the tours was running really late and may not make it to Chelsea in time. *A-hem* I could do it? Really? Yeah, I've been on loads now and have learnt the script to go with it. Well, maybe then.

Eventually, the guy did turn up and we did do the tour together. However, as a special thank you, I was given the keys and told I could give my dad a private tour of Stamford Bridge. WOW!!! When my Dad turned up I did exactly that, including telling him the story of meeting Ken Bates and Ruud Gullit earlier!

I can't imagine anything like this happening nowadays but will always have the memories to tell my children when they are older. Up the Chels!

A season ticket holder at Stamford Bridge, Chelsea Chadder is something of a Twitter phenomenon with over 100,000 followers. He has also written several popular books about The Blues. You can find out more by following him @ChelseaChadder

SILVERWARE BLUES
Neil Smith

Although my beloved Football Club have experienced some great success over the last few years, winning their first FA Cup followed by the European Cup Winners' Cup in 1970 and 1971 I have yet to be present when a trophy has been secured much to my despair.

In April 1970 I was at Wembley to witness the first tied Cup Final in many, many years but unfortunately was not allowed to go to the replay at Old Trafford, Manchester upon the guidance of my loving parents who would have had to fund my trip anyway! That said Ian Hutchinson's headed equaliser with only four minutes remaining after we had just gone 2-1 down still makes the hairs on the back of my neck stand on end.

I had obtained my FA Cup Final ticket by attending every home league game and then pasting the coupons from the back page of the official programme onto an application form which was then sent by Registered Mail together with a postal order for ten shillings and a stamped self addressed envelope. I attended the game with my father, brother, uncle and two cousins.

Much to my chagrin tickets for the replay were obtained purely by queueing at Stamford Bridge on the Sunday morning prior to the game on the Wednesday evening...first come first served.

This meant that some classmates and neighbours who had not been at Wembley witnessed the fantastic event whilst I watched it on TV... exuberant but gutted not to be there.

Mother even relented and agreed that the following day I could skip school and journey up to the ground for the homecoming victory parade. However arriving at Rayners Lane Station from Uxbridge there was a signal failure and I eventually arrived at the Bridge as thousands were returning joyously with the team having long departed from Fulham Town Hall.

The following season I again attended every home game and have vivid memories in particular of the European Cup Winners Cup ties played under floodlights.

In the First Round the Greek club, Aris Salonika, were easily despatched 6-2 on aggregate. After a 1-1 draw in Greece the return leg saw Chelsea really turn on the style winning 5-1. John Hollins netted twice the second being an absolute screamer from all of thirty yards. Hutchinson also got a brace and the fifth came from Marvin Hinton on a rare forage forward after a couple of neat one-twos.

Next up were the Bulgarian Army side CSKA Sofia. Although a tougher task than the previous round the Blues became the first team to beat them on their home soil in European competition with a goal from Tommy Baldwin just before half time. The second leg was no formality either with Peter Bonetti making two saves as good as any in his illustrious career before a scrambled effort from David Webb secured the tie on a 2-0 aggregate.

Into the quarter-finals Chelsea were pitted against the Belgian team FC Bruges. By all accounts the first away leg was a bruising encounter both on and off the pitch. Two goals before half time from the hosts went unanswered and the team struggled without the suspended Peter Osgood. The following Saturday when attending our league fixture at Tottenham I learned first-hand from many present in Belgium of police brutality evidenced by contusions from batons and even scars from dog bites.

We eagerly awaited the return leg praying that Ossie would be fit after missing ten games. On the night we were relieved to hear that the King of Stamford Bridge would indeed start the match. I took up my usual vantage point from the terrace between the Bovril Entrance and the West Stand where we would lever ourselves up and cling from the fencing above the bench seating to obtain a decent view of proceedings.

Just before kick-off the hundred or so visiting supporters from Belgium made their presence known noisily entering the rear of the West Stand adjacent to us.

During the ensuing "banter" between us one youth alongside me flicked his cigarette end into the visitors throng where it landed on top of a Belgian's felt fedora and unbeknown to the recipient began to smoulder. Within a minute or so the hat went up in flames accompanied by our raucous laughter. A policeman then lectured the miscreant but had difficulty keeping a straight face whilst doing so. No arrest made, no ejection and thankfully no injury sustained.

On the pitch Chelsea played a quite superb game with Alan Hudson, in particular, dominating although every man was a hero. Peter Houseman had steered in a first-half effort and just before the interval Ron Harris despatched a piledriver which amazingly appeared to strike the foot of both posts before bouncing out of play.

With less than ten minutes remaining Osgood netted at the North End before leaping the dog track and celebrating with pursuing ball boys and peanut sellers. Extra-time saw another superb Osgood goal after a mesmerising dribble and lay back by Hudson followed by a fourth from Baldwin. It was certainly the best atmosphere and game I had experienced in my five years at Stamford Bridge.

The semi-final paired Chelsea with holders Manchester City who worryingly had trounced us 3-0 at home in the Fourth Round of the FA Cup aided by a supreme performance from England International midfielder Colin Bell who netted twice. However Bell was now struggling with injury and would not appear in either leg. Osgood, too, was to miss both games through injury and his strike partner, Hutchinson, had already been ruled out for the rest of the season.

In the first tie at the Bridge Chelsea edged a 1-0 win courtesy of a fine strike from the young South African, Derek Smethurst, filling in for a rare appearance in Osgood's absence. John Boyle, playing at right-back, was denied an obvious penalty late in the game when clearly tripped.

Chelsea journeyed north for the second leg and with both teams still decimated through injuries the bookies favoured City to make the final. However Chelsea had other ideas and although Smethurst had an early effort ruled out for offside reached the final by way of an own goal from City keeper Ron Healey who palmed Keith Weller's indirect free kick into his own net. Boyle, appearing this time in the number ten shirt in midfield, was undoubtedly the man of the match.

The game was 12 months to the day after the FA Cup Final triumph and, once again, I was denied the opportunity to attend. In the weeks leading up to the final in Athens the official programme advertised charter trips via the tour company 4S travel at £35. I asked my parents if they would fund my trip and I would repay them at £1 per week from my paper round earnings. After considering my request for a good two minutes the request was declined.

So on May 19, 1971 the family gathered in the living room to listen to radio coverage of the final as amazingly the BBC were broadcasting the Home International fixture between England and Wales live from Wembley. My memory of the evening is vague and all I can really recall is the commentator relaying that the trophy had been placed pitch-side ready for presentation to the victorious Chelsea side when Real Madrid equalised in the dying moments after Osgood had given Chelsea the lead around the hour mark.

And so to bed. However there was better news in the morning when we learned that the replay in Athens would be shown live by the BBC the following evening. At school on Thursday fans of rival teams sniggered at me and said our chance had gone and, again, the bookies favoured our opponents.

Chelsea though came up trumps putting in a superb performance and securing their first European trophy with a fine 2-1 win courtesy of goals from John Dempsey and Osgood again.

After viewing the game and trophy presentation my brother and I donned our blue and white scarves and hastily headed off to the village cricket club where we teamed up with other local Chelsea fans. Whilst I was not allowed entrance to the licenced bar my elders passed a number of bottles of cider to me from inside the pavilion and at closing time we noisily toasted our Club's success with renditions of every Blues anthem we knew.

Arriving home my Mother declared that I was drunk and after we all retired she spent the best part of the night patrolling the landing in case i was ill. Thankfully I made it through the night and in the morning we set off for the Bridge to witness the triumphant homecoming.

Upon arrival at the Bridge my elders all beat a hasty retreat to the Britannia public house whereas my mate Steve and I entered a block of flats adjacent to the Supporters Club shop and secured a viewing position from above the Trattoria below. Hours passed and thousands upon thousands assembled in the streets below and every vantage point on top of the buildings around us became occupied. Then at around 4pm a deafening crescendo greeted the open-top bus with the players parading the Cup. Although Eddie McCreadie had missed the final through injury it was his eyes that met mine as he thrust the trophy towards us. Down below I witnessed my cousin Brian trampled under the hooves of a police horse but thankfully returning to his feet still smiling!

Maybe before too long I will actually be present in a stadium following Chelsea securing yet another trophy?

Neil Smith is the author of 'The A to Z of Chelsea: Where Were You When We Were Shocking?' and the co-author of 'Eddie Mac, Eddie Mac: Life and times at Chelsea under Eddie McCreadie'. He compiles a monthly trivia quiz for the 'cfcuk' fanzine and can be found on Twitter @SmiffyEastStand

WORLD CHAMPIONS
Chris Axon

Foxy, PD and I caught a cab to the game, though the cabbie took us initially to the city's other football stadium where the third and fourth place play-off was due to start. Luckily, the correct stadium was only five minutes away. The crowds were far greater than on Wednesday. The three of us were allocated tickets in the lower tier of the western end of the stadium, the section used by the Al Hilal support previously. There was quite a wait to reach the security checks. Palmeiras fans again dominated; the green and white was everywhere. I noted how many of the Brazilians had adopted the local Arabic headgear, again in green and white.

"Can't see that catching on among our lot to be honest."

My Alhosn App had gone grey where it ought to have been green, but I was waved through.

Then, a personal hell.

A "jobsworth" told me that I had to hand in my small camera. His supervisor said the same. I kicked up a bit of a fuss and they went off to see another supervisor. Thankfully, another chap allowed me to take it in.

"Thank you my friend."

In an exact copy of Wednesday, we were in with an hour to go.

Inside, my first thoughts were dominated by the realisation that there was no worthwhile segregation present in the entire stadium. How easy would it have been for FIFA to have given us one stand? It annoyed me because not only were around 10,000 Palmeiras fans crammed in at the other end (although, mysteriously, with a little section of around three hundred Chelsea fans in one corner), our area was adjacent to a section with around 5,000 Palmeiras fans. I wasn't worried about it kicking off at all – far from it – but I just wanted a solid block of Chelsea so that we could noisily get behind the team.

I spotted many people that I recognised in our section. As kick-off time approached, the ground swelled. The lower tier of the western end really was full to bursting, the central section especially. It looked like this was the home of their ultras, "La Manche Verde" – the green spot – and many seemed to be wearing special edition white shirts.

The minutes ticked by.

Throughout, the Brazilians were in fine voice. Many songs were aired. One chant dominated:

"Pal – meeeeeeeiiiiiiiiiiir – as."

With the middle syllable stretched out forever.
We were pretty quiet at this stage; outnumbered and out sung.
I looked around.

Foxy was a few rows in front. Mike and Frank were down the front. Close by were the South Gloucestershire contingent, the couples Liz and Mark, Karen and Feisal. My good mate Andy from Nuneaton was there too. Welsh Kev called over for a photo. Over in the corner I spotted Big Rich who had suffered for a day or two after being given a positive test result on arrival. Thankfully he tested negative soon after and was able to attend both games. He was with a few people I recognised; Darren, Ryan, Denise, Andy, Rob. King Kenny and Rob were there. Then in the front row of the side stand, the North Stand, I spotted Della and Mick, Clinton who had flown in for the final – along with Tombsie who I saw outside – and Darren and Leigh.

There was a hundred or so Chelsea fans, dressed all in blue – how quaint – from the local Dubai supporters' group. JD had mentioned a large contingent from Kerala in India at the Al Hilal match; they were here too surely.

There was more "Chelsea – are you ready?" hoopla (no, let's just call it "bollocks") but at least it managed to quieten down the Brazilians.

With kick-off approaching, the stadium lights were dimmed and some fearsome fireworks exploded into the sky.

Then, the teams.
Chelsea in blue / blue / white.
Palmeiras in white / white / green.

Thomas Tuchel, himself only just returned to the fold after a bout of COVID, chose these players to bring home the...er, bacon in the Abu Dhabi night.

Mendy
Christensen – Silva – Rudiger
Azpilicueta - Kovacic – Kante – Hudson-Odoi
Mount – Havertz
Lukaku

"Big night for Callum."

How many Chelsea fans were in the stadium? It was so difficult to hazard a guess. Maybe 4,000 all told? Who knows? Maybe slightly more than 15,000 Palmeiras? That leaves around 12,000 neutrals? But how many of those neutrals, I spotted shirts of the other competing teams, were supporting us? No idea.

The game began.

From the off, it was obvious that Palmeiras were more than happy to let us have the ball. And we had it in spades. I was amazed how far Thiago Silva was allowed to carry the ball; over the half-way line and beyond. In modern parlance, this was a very low block.

Off the pitch, the Brazilian fans were on fire. Their noise dominated. Curls of white paper cascaded down from the Palmeiras fans above me in the upper tier. It felt like we were in a hornets' nest.

Palmeiras enjoyed a couple of half-chances but Mendy was not bothered. On ten minutes, Kai Havertz to Callum Hudson-Odoi but his shot was blocked. On twenty-two minutes, Mount misjudged the pace of the ball as it dropped into the six-yard box and he let it run on. Soon after, two shots from Havertz were screwed wide.

Out of nowhere, a lightning break from Palmeiras but the aptly named Dudu slapped his shot well wide. It was, however, the half's biggest chance. Sadly, on the thirty-minute mark, Mount was injured and was replaced by Christian Pulisic. I was honestly surprised that Ziyech was not given the nod. Every time that Silva advanced, I just wanted him to go another five or ten yards, drop his shoulder and rattle in a shot on goal. At last, a few moments before half-time, he did just that. The beautifully named Weverton leapt to force it around the post for a corner.

Half-time came with the game scoreless.

Although we were finding it hard to break down this Palmeiras side, I was relieved. I was relieved that they were clearly not as able as I had presumed them to be.

At half-time, more "bollocks" as the lights were dimmed and spectators were asked to shine their mobile torches. It brought me immense pleasure to see one corner of the stadium not joining in.

It was akin to the blackout during the Second World War, for those who enjoy such hyperbole.

The second-half began and maybe noticing that the Palmeiras fans were in a moment of quiet and rest, the Chelsea corner were roused and our loudest chant of the night cheered me.

"Chelsea – Chelsea – Chelsea – Chelsea – Chelsea – Chelsea – Chelsea."

Good ol' "Amazing Grace."

Other teams mock us when we sing that, but it's ours and ours alone.

A Rudiger rocket was blasted at goal. We continued to dominate. The ball was played out to Hudson-Odoi on our left. He had not enjoyed a great game thus far to be honest. I bellowed at him :

"Come on Callum, dig it out."

Well, dig it out he did.

His cross was well hit, on the money, and a bullet header from Lukaku at the near post sent us all delirious.

Just after, a shot from Pulisic was drilled just wide.

"Ooooooooh."

A very rare attack on our goal followed within ten minutes of our goal. The ball was lofted into the box from a throw-in and a shot was smothered by Mendy with ease. The moment passed. But then some commotion and some noise. There was a VAR review.

"Bollocks."

The penalty was given and I had no complaints after seeing the replay; Thiago Silva's arm was up at an angle, a definite penalty.

Raphael Veiga converted.

Game on.

We drifted a little now, our impetus broken a little. But we still carved out chances with Havertz and Pulisic going close.

Timo Werner replaced Lukaku and Saul replaced Hudson-Odoi on seventy-six minutes. To be fair, their fresh legs helped us. We turned up the heat but Palmeiras defended well.

With five minutes to go, fresh green and white vertical streamers were held aloft over the lower tier of the end opposite. I guess this was to spur their team on in the last portion of the game. I always remember that we used to sing "Chelsea" to "Amazing Grace" during most second-halves back in the 'eighties. It was "our thing."

The last kick of normal time saw Mateo Kovacic blast high over the bar.

We settled our nerves for an extra thirty minutes and – gasp – possible penalties. Foxy came and stood with PD and little old me.

"Hope you're our good luck charm, mate."

Into extra-time we went.

Malang Sarr for Christensen.

Hakim Ziyech for Kovacic.

I had been standing for hours. My "lucky" yellow Adidas trainers – Porto – were starting to pinch. I was tired and weary.

"Come on Chels."

More Chelsea domination, more Palmeiras resistance. A rare Palmeiras break, but Rudiger held firm with a sensational shoulder charge. He had been exceptional all game. I spotted rows of Palmeiras fans in the opposite end gently swaying from side to side. Another sight that you don't see back home.

Into the second period of extra time we went. The night was drawing on. And to think that one of my initial travel options had been to catch a 2.55am flight home on Sunday morning.

We found new life again. Werner wriggled and went close. The game became tense. I willed us on.

"Come on you blue boys."

With only four minutes remaining, a Ziyech corner was swung into the box. It was knocked down and Dave swung at it. There was a block from a defender and the three or four nearest Chelsea defenders instantly appealed for a handball. Play continued but when the ball went out of play, the referee signalled for another VAR review. PD and Foxy was adamant that we'd get the decision. The Australian referee again trotted off to look at the pitch side screen.

Penalty.

I loathe VAR but I could not resist a yelp of joy.

Then ensued pure drama. Dave, the one who had won the penalty, the captain, claimed the ball. My immediate thoughts?

Dave? Shades of JT in Moscow. Oh bloody hell. Brave man.

The Palmeiras players were in Dave's face for ages. Or what seemed like it. Then, a dialogue with Timo. Give it to him? Not my choice. Then, the last twist; Dave calmly handed the ball to Kai Havertz, the hero in Porto.

A moment of calm.

A moment of drama.

I held my camera ready.

The run up.

Click.

He sent the 'keeper the wrong way, shades of Didier in Munich, the ball flew in.

YES!

I yelled with joy and looked to the sky. But I then became light-headed. By the time I had steadied myself, Havertz had run to the Chelsea corner and was being mobbed by everyone.

Click, click, click.

Joy.

Joy.

Joy.

The Palmeiras fans were quiet now. The Chelsea section was buzzing.

One last twist; the Palmeiras player Luan, after another delay, was sent off for wiping out Havertz the scorer. Just after the resulting free-kick was taken, the referee blew.

At around 11.20pm on a balmy night in Abu Dhabi, Chelsea Football Club became World Champions.

Fackinell.

Chris Axon is a home and away Chelsea season ticket holder whose fascinating and wonderfully-written blog about his travels watching The Blues over land and sea really is essential weekly reading. Chelsea/esque (A Blue World In Black And White) can be found at https://caxonblog.com

HOME IS WHERE THE HEART IS
David Chidgey

Some people have a remarkable memory for matches. I am not one of those people.

I have always been in awe of the likes of Kelvin Barker, Walter Otton, Mark Worrall, Neil 'Smiffy' Smith and Mark Meehan, not just for their superb writing, but for their ability to remember, in granular detail, events from Chelsea matches going back 40 years and more.

I, on the other hand, can barely remember details from a match last week. I used to blame the amount of beer I drank before and after a match, but in truth, it's not just that.

I do remember the first time I visited Stamford Bridge though. April 3, 1976. Sadly, this was not a match to feature Chelsea. In fact, I hadn't really found Chelsea at the age of 10, not having been born into it like so many of my Chelsea friends.

For some reason that I still don't quite understand, my Dad had got hold of two tickets for the FA Cup semi-final between Southampton and Crystal Palace. So off we went to one of my first trips to London from the 'Boondocks' of mid-Hampshire.

I can still picture clearly the walk from Fulham Broadway, the massed crowd all drawn to the somewhat ramshackle but spacious Stamford Bridge. The evocative smell of hot dogs, onions and horse manure; the scarf, badge and programme sellers. It was quite simply a brilliant sensory overload or as we now know it the match-day experience.

Inside the ground I found myself in the front of the Shed halfway between the penalty area and the corner flag. I even saw Brian Moore the ITV commentator make his way up to the commentary position in the West Stand. In truth, I was more transfixed by the stadium than the match itself. In fact, I was transfixed by the relatively new East Stand that had only been open for a couple of years. For a 10-year-old, it looked like some incongruous spaceship had landed in a football ground, so huge and out of character with the rest of the ground did it appear.

And, for me, that was where it all really started. The team I would follow from then on would be Chelsea. It would take me nearly ten years to return, which I did thanks to going to the University of London and living in Chelsea in the mid 1980's.

Having never acquired the match going habit, I was never a regular attender in those days. I only finally got a season ticket 21-years ago when I made a pact with my then brother-in-law, Martin Levy (Dr. Mart on the Chelsea FanCast), that I would do so when I moved back to London, which I did in 2001.

While the memories from the 80's and 90's are hazy (in more ways than one), the last 20-odd years are a little clearer. What memories they are too, happily coinciding with the arrival of Roman Abramovich and the most successful period in the Club's history.

In fact, there are just too many great memories of games, people and hilarious incidents to choose a definitive one. But in no particular order...

The surreal matches against Barcelona. Sitting in the Shed Upper with Dr. Mart as Frank Lampard, Damien Duff and Eidur Gudjohnsen tore into the Catalans to score three goals in nine minutes in 2005.

The infamous 1-1 in 2009 when Michael Essien's screamer was cancelled out by a last-minute Andreas Iniesta goal and the appalling refereeing of Tom Henning Ovrebo. I have never been so angry at a match and had I been able to launch myself from the back of Gate 17 to drop kick Ovrebo, I would not have hesitated.

And then the poetic justice, set up by a typical Didier Drogba goal in the 2012 semi-final. I was near the front in the West Lower, by the goal line, and had a perfect view of Drogba knee-sliding towards me.

Controversial Champions League games were not just the preserve of Barcelona though. I was privileged to witness some barnstormers against Liverpool too, such as the 4-4 draw in 2009 which clinched a semi-final place against the aforementioned Barcelona. Sitting in the Matthew Upper that night, behind the goal, the noise at the final whistle and the jumping up and down to 'One Step Beyond' physically moved the tier, bouncing up and down by a few feet.

For pure hilarity, the 6-0 against Arsenal in March 2014 is numero uno. Arsene Wenger's 1000th match in charge of Arsenal completely ruined. Wenger losing his cool with Mourinho. Chelsea 3-0 up inside 17-minutes and the hapless Andre Marriner sending off Kieran Gibbs having mistaken him for the real offender Alex Oxlade-Chamberlain. Honestly, I have never laughed out loud at a football match as much as I did that day. To add to the hilarity, Mo Salah, a serial under-achiever for Chelsea, scored the sixth.

Talking of the joy of six, one of the most peculiar matches I've seen at the Bridge was in October 2007 when Chelsea played Manchester City. I think in those days we were drinking in either the Wheatsheaf or the Jolly Maltster pub before matches. Dr. Mart thought it would be a great idea to see how many pints of Stella Artois he could get me to drink before the match. I managed to down six before we set off to our seats in Gate 17.

I think I would have been pretty raucous, fuelled by the Stella, had Chelsea played out a dull 0-0 draw. The Blues had other ideas and put The Citizens to the sword with a scintillating display of attacking football and put six past goalie Joe Hart. Dr. Mart was convinced it was my 'Stella' performance rather than Chelsea's stellar performance that was responsible for the six goals and attempted to repeat the feat for the next few matches. It didn't work though as neither Chelsea nor I were able to reprise the performance.

If I was to choose just one match that had absolutely everything that encompasses the experience of watching Chelsea at Stamford Bridge, it would be the Champions League match against Napoli in March 2012.

The Blues were up against it and looked favourites to go out having lost 3-1 to Napoli in the away leg two weeks prior. By the time of the return leg, Andre Villas-Boas and his doomed project had hit the rocks and he had been given his P45. Chelsea legend, Roberto Di Matteo had taken the reins which was about the only hopeful spot in a season which looked like unravelling.

My personal life was in a similar position. My company had gone bust in January owing a considerable amount of money and I personally had lost about a year's salary. To say I was skint was an understatement. In fact, I hadn't been able to afford to buy a ticket for the match.

Nevertheless, I was determined to be in the manor for the game to soak up some of the pre-match atmosphere, meet a few mates and then was resigned to slope off to watch the match in a local pub.

I was talking to Marco at the 'cfcuk' stall when my phone rang. When I answered, the West Country burr of Dave Jones, one of the Swindon Blues was on the other end. He had a ticket for sale if I wanted it and could I meet him in the pub in 20-minutes? I thanked him but said I didn't have £40 so wouldn't be able to, but I'd meet him in the pub anyway.

I trudged off bemoaning my luck but 10-minutes later the phone rang again. This time it was Marco animatingly exclaiming that he'd just sold two Chelsea FanCast T-shirts and if I hurried up, I could grab the £40 from him, meet Dave and purchase the ticket with my name on it.

Amazing, now in funds, 'Chidgerella' was going to the ball.

Little did we know then that the next 120-minutes of football was to be one of the most dramatic in the Club's history. Very few teams come back from 3-1 down to get through a Champions League tie. The match ebbed and flowed, but the Chelsea supporters were vocal and loud and four-square behind the team all night. It was tense mind, but thankfully the stadium disc jockey had the sense to play Bob Marley's 'Three Little Birds' before extra-time. It helped, and indeed everything turned out alright!

What ensued at the final whistle, with Chelsea going through by virtue of a Brana Ivanovic goal, right in front of us in The Shed on 105-minutes was utter madness, quite literally, as we all skanked ecstatically to 'One Step Beyond'.

An unforgettable night. One of the best ever. And none of it would have happened to me without the generosity and thoughtfulness of good Chelsea mates. To say I am indebted would be an understatement.

But that's what it's always been about hasn't it. The 'cfcuk' stall, the pubs, the people, the characters, the faces in the stadium. The people who you bump into that you've known for years and those you speak with at most matches whose names you don't even know. It's all about the connection to the place, the people, the community, and it feels like one big family.

Following Chelsea is like having a second family and to me, Stamford Bridge is like a second home, a home where the heart most definitely resides. If you put that in the context of the Trust's 'Sleep Out' initiative to help the homeless, it certainly makes you realise just how lucky some of us are, win or lose, rain or shine.

David Chidgey aka 'Stamford Chidge' aka 'The Podfather' is the host of the 'long-running 'Chelsea Fancast' podcast which is broadcast live on Monday's and Friday's during the football season. Chidge works as a Psychodynamic Counsellor and is an integral part of the team behind 'Over The Line' and education and signposting service to help Chelsea fans through difficult times. Follow him on Twitter @StamfordChidge

PERFECT MATCH
Paul Radcliffe

FRANK MILLER used to be a giant. Born at the turn of the century, he and his world had become smaller by the 1980s.

As he waited for his grandson he sat inside his heavy overcoat on a tired armchair. Dust motes hung in the sunlight spilling through the rear window with its splintered frame and cracked glass. He was a patient man and knew he was ready too early. But what else was there to do on this fine day?

Last night I dreamt I was going to Stamford Bridge again, he allowed himself a wry smile. Except it wasn't a dream, today he would be strolling down the Fulham Road like he had done on hundreds of Saturdays, but this time with Sam and his friends.

It was decent of them to offer him a ticket. After all he hadn't been to a game for years, before he retired in fact. He was sure the lads, all in their twenties, didn't want an old man around wasting valuable drinking time. But Sam had been adamant so he felt obliged to accept.

The Victorian-style carriage clock on the soot-blackened mantelpiece had been a gift after 49 years' service with London Underground. As station master at Tooting Bec and Tooting Broadway he had run his domain with painstaking, some said pedantic, efficiency.

Standing six-foot-four with a beer belly to match, Frank had been an imposing figure. Virtually bald in his forties he had opted for a number one cut which gave him a mask of menace despite his sparkling blue eyes and the laughter lines etched on his face.

Frank's decaying terraced home was in one of the roads known as the Apostles, part of an old estate in Raynes Park. The street was an eclectic mix of gentrified houses with loft conversions and two-up two-downs with outside lavatories.

Sam pushed the front door open, on the latch as always. 'Granddad please keep the door locked, it's not safe,' said Sam as he loped into the sitting room and folded himself onto another chair. Frank shrugged. She does as she pleases, he brooded forlornly.

"What have you done to yourself?" said Sam gesturing towards Frank's face where a black eye was still just about noticeable.

"Oh, nothing, stumbled into the door frame. I'd forgotten about it."

"Looks nasty, did you go to the doctor?"

"Pointless, you can't see him for weeks," said Frank. "Anyway let's get going. Where are we meeting the boys?"

The house was bitterly cold. Frank had a tartan blanket covered in spills and crumbs over his lap and around his scrawny legs. His breathing was laboured and he had two asthma inhalers beside him.

The downstairs rooms had been knocked through years earlier, but now as the relationship between the couple became bleaker, a version of the Berlin Wall was in place. The divide was marked by a grey blanket on a washing line which was tied to hooks on either side of the room.

"Do you fancy some soup before we go?" said Sam inoffensively, avoiding eye contact through the over-long fringe of his new romantic hair style.

"Soup," said Frank with undisguised derision. "A large scotch is what I need, sunshine, not a bowl of minestrone."

Nan's side of the barrier was cluttered with magazines, playing cards, bags of second-hand clothes and bric-a-brac, seaside trinkets from Blackpool to Barcelona and packs of postcards held together by rubber bands – written by strangers to strangers.

"Where's Nan today?" asked Sam.

"Jumble sale or whist drive, I suppose,"said Frank mildly. "Somewhere she can't see me. Or hear me."

"How's Lester been treating you recently granddad?" asked Sam as they left the house.

"Not bad at all," said Frank. "We had 7-2 and 2-1 winners yesterday. Paid for my rolling tobacco."

Frank's betting method was to put £1 to win on Lester Piggott whenever the champion jockey rode. His morning routine took in the betting shop, the newsagent for his copy of the Daily Express and the café at the end of his road. As far as Sam was aware that was his granddad's life.

In the underpass near the station there was what looked like a pile of old rags and a mud spattered black rucksack in the puddles of gloom. But as the men drew nearer a freckled face appeared from the shadows and said, "Pound for a cup of tea, mister?"

The girl looked about 17. She had greasy, short ginger hair, red rimmed bulging eyes and cold sores around her nose and mouth. Her front teeth were cracked and she smelled of urine, stale beer and takeaway fries. She wore dirty white trainers that were too big for her, ripped black jeans that exposed her red knees and layers of tops under a battered, green army surplus jacket.

As Sam clumsily rummaged in the pocket of his baggy Levi's looking for a £1 coin, Frank stepped forward and asked her name.

"What's it matter to you?' she said, 'You don't get my life story for a quid."

The men seemed to loom over her in the dark recesses of the tunnel so she stood up. About five foot tall, pale and prickly.

"Just asking, no offence intended,'"said Frank mildly.

"Some taken," she said.

"We're locals. I've lived here all my life. What about you?," asked Frank.

"Stockport. Looking for work. I'm a dancer."

"I'm Frank and this is my grandson, Sam," said Frank. He took his elegant leather wallet from his jacket pocket and gave her a £20 note. "You take care now."

"Oh," she said quietly, "You're not perverts then. Many thanks." She wiped her snotty nose with her sleeve, picked up her meagre belongings and was gone.

"That was generous granddad," said Sam. "Not really, just don't like the thought of anyone having to sleep rough," Frank murmured.

They took the train, then a packed District Line tube clattered from Wimbledon to Fulham Broadway where they joined the Chelsea faithful as they clambered up the footbridge stairs and through the arcade of old shops.

At the Jolly Maltster, Sam nodded to the two skinhead bouncers. Both in their thirties, they looked dangerous. They were granted entry through the side door into a seething mass of bodies four deep at the bar with The Clash pulsating from the stereo speakers. In the far corner Nick looking like a refugee from Stalin's gulags and Easty, in the loudest Hawaiian shirt ever made, had managed to secure a table in the corner. Sam guided his frail granddad through the forest of limbs to the table where Easty gave up his seat to the older man.

"All on lager boys?" said Sam turning back to the melee.

"And a large vodka, while you're up there," said Nick, trying his luck.

Sam eventually managed to edge to the bar and was served by a brunette with a scrunchy black hairband. She looked tired and thoroughly bored by the whole experience. Back at the table Frank said, 'Did I ever tell you that I brought my old dear to a game when we were courting? 65,000 fellers in the crowd plus Nan. It was February in the 1921/22 season, Buchanan Sharp scored the only goal as we destroyed Cardiff City 1-0. Terrible game and she absolutely hated it.

"Still, she must have thought something of me back then because we were married six months later."

Beer followed beer and story followed story spanning decades supporting the club. As 3pm drew near the men made their way through the crowded streets to the hubbub of the West Stand with its familiar aroma of leather jackets, cigarette smoke and beer. Just 12,736 fans watched a 3-0 victory over Oldham courtesy of a Tony McAndrew penalty and goals from Kerry Dixon and David Speedie. Only 200 away fans on the old North Stand terrace. No trouble, no problem.

After the game and another few rounds, Sam guided his granddad back home. Still no sign of his Nan but Frank seemed relaxed and ten years younger than earlier in the day. Sam left him studying the match programme and waiting for 'Match of the Day'.

Two weeks later Sam turned the corner into his Granddad's road ready to complete the whole ritual again. A clamour of rooks sat in silence on the pitched roof of his Granddad's home and he was shocked to see a police squad car with blue lights strobing parked at an angle in the road.

He strode into the house where an officer in the cramped hall stopped him but he had already glimpsed the dreadful scene. Frank sat slumped in his chair with the Express open at the racing pages. His head was pushed back at an unnatural angle. Blood oozed down his face and neck from a hideous series of wounds where his forehead and eye socket had been caved in.

On the other side of the Berlin blanket his Nan, a sturdy woman with blue hair and a big old fashioned hearing aid, sat in an upright chair in front of the blank television screen as an officer carried out a bagged, heavy walking stick covered in sticky blackness.

Paul Radcliffe has supported Chelsea for almost 50 years. His first book, 'Blue Hitmen: Chelsea's 25 Greatest Goals' was published in 2021. You can follow Paul on Twitter @PaulRadcliffeFC

SAME PLACE, DIFFERENT STADIUM
Charles Rose

You never forget your first time. April 16, 1968. 3pm Saturday afternoon. Having got fed up of his son dragging him to watch Southern League football, and failing to get him interested in the main town sport of Rugby, here I was going to a big game at a big ground and watching a big team.

Why I support Chelsea is simple. My Dad knew how to get to Stamford Bridge.

Our tickets were in the old (but still then referred to as the new) West Stand. Getting in seemed like climbing the Eiger, up a vertiginous set of steps. In those pre-Ibrox disaster days in straight lines. At the top the odd tea bar, and then the entrances into the stand with the wooden seats. That first view stays with you. The amazing expanse of green, the buzz of anticipation and crowd noise. The smell of gently frying hot dog onions, and an earthy male smell emanating from the crowd and in particular the basic facilities.

The rest of the ground still bore the outline of the original bowl design from the beginning of the century, built on the slag from the railway. The open end with the rather strange small North Stand in the corner. Opposite was the main East Stand with its high up viewing box so famously used by The Doc when urging on his "Diamonds". Designed by the go to Scottish architect Archibald Leitch, it was a thing of its time and a certain beauty. At its highest point the weathervane, depicting George 'Gatling Gun' Hilsdon. There were many other examples of his fine work from Villa Park, to Goodison, to Roker to Rangers in the North. They were stands of beauty, frequently and unlike ours double decker stands. None of these stands survive, indeed many of the grounds are now housing estates or shopping centres.

At the South, the most iconic of Chelsea locations The Shed. In truth a basic covering that started just to the west of the steps up and went along to the the Bovril Entrance. Basic maybe but the beating heart of Stamford Bridge.

The West Stand was built in 1965 before my time, and contained Executive Boxes at the top, some of the first of their kind. Even then the ideas of sitting in little more than a glorified glass box did not appeal. The seats were hard and relatively small, and the stand went to about two-thirds of the way towards the pitch. From there in there were benches which you could upgrade to on the day of the game.

As a ground it was to me a revelation. Used to a ground where the home crowd moved to change ends at half-time, and crowds of 2000 to 4000, this was everything I had dreamed of and more. It was the beginning of a love affair with the architecture of football grounds. Each away trip those years later accompanied by Simon Inglis' methodical book 'The Football Grounds of Great Britain'. Unlike many of our newer grounds, some of which are mere copy and paste replicas, there were real points of difference. In this city alone The Shelf and Clock End in the North, the Chicken Run in the East each had their own mythical status. From the sublime to the ridiculous you had the massive ends in Birmingham and Liverpool while at Luton one side was made up of a stand called Bobbers. It had a walkway at the back which proved to be the scene of a dangerous encounter in the 1970s.

Rather like the characters playing then, from a distance they appear more interesting, less programmed and somehow less sterile. They played football with a degree of firmness bordering on violence. Off the field there was a firm drinking culture.

That stadium layout saw some of the most atmospheric performances I can remember. The season we won the FA Cup in 1970, I had seen us play Leeds in what was the first classic I saw at the Bridge. One down we fought back with goals by Osgood and Hollins to lead at half time. The excitement and noise was a revelation. In the second half Chelsea were shown up by the best team in the land, as Leeds scored four without reply. It is never great seeing your team beaten, but when the other side outplays you and indeed is of that class then that is another thing altogether. It was chosen by Match of the Day as the game of the season.

A mere five years later the disastrous renovation project on hold and the team relegated to Division 2, we faced Sunderland in the league just before Christmas. My fellow traveller, Buster and I took the opportunity to do a little shopping on the way to the game rather than indulge in underage drinking. His great idea, was to purchase a porcelain plate which he guarded up his jumper. My memories were of a boisterous crowd that as usual surged and swayed in the Shed. We surged and swayed with them, as each chorus of "Knees up Mother Brown" enveloped our end. When the late and lamented Ian Britton scored, The Shed went into spasms. As we guarded the present between us, thinking only of the plate we moved a goodly distance down the terrace. All part of the fun.

By that stage the East Stand we know of today was built. Lionised in a rather effete architectural analysis on BBC 2 a few years ago as a modern classic, many may wish to differ. As an integral part of a wider redevelopment it sits alone as a monument to our lofty but misplaced ambition. It almost cost everything.

The pulsating games of that era were generally in the lower division. The Shed became a battle ground for opposing fans, who tried and occasionally "took" the end, in the same way that our fans did at their grounds. Two episodes stick out in my mind, from 1977, when in quick succession both West Ham and Millwall appeared in the middle to cause mayhem. Cue horses on the pitch and as I recall it actually on the terrace itself. Once cleared out the walk of shame/triumph past the rest of the crowd to join their motley crew ensured. I recall the Millwall game finishing and as both fans wore blue and white bar scarves, (that's right no writing folks) no one could tell who was who? As I made a tactical change of route my last sight was of one of our own having his face thrust rather aggressively against a side window of a van, full of police who looked indifferent until they decided to come out swinging. That violence was an every-match occurrence in that era, one that is fortunately well behind us.

Not all our derby games were so afflicted. The Boxing Day game in 1976 (actually on December 27) against Fulham attracted over 55,000. They were hanging off the hoardings at the North Stand end and it felt and was a memorable day. Fulham boasting Best, Marsh, and Moore, we the young bucks with Wilkins, Swain, and Langley giving them a proper game which we won 2-0.

As our league form was the usual mixture of erratic and wasteful. I never saw us mount a proper challenge for the First Division title only the league below. In the run up to that Fulham game, we played top of the table Wolverhampton Wanderers in front of 36,000-plus including legendary American Politician Henry Kissinger, who unlike many Americans and indeed politicians did actually understand and love the game. The footage of that game including commentary from the legendary Brian Moore for ITV's 'The Big Match', captures the wonderful atmosphere as we fought back from 3-1 down to equalise in the last minutes through Steve 'Jock' Finnieston. What you can also see is the rubble of the North Stand and hear the crowd chanting, "Chelsea Aggro... hello, hello". As the fighting continued (according to Moore) so did the game. It was a usual occurrence. The Shed pulsated and urged the team on. It was said that when that third goal went in, the US security service immediately surrounded Mr Kissinger for fear that an assassination was being planned!

In those barren years, the FA Cup provided some comfort. Two victories over Liverpool through the genius of on the first occasion of Clive Walker and on the second through Peter Rhodes-Brown gave us hope. Hope that inevitably was dashed. The Fifth Round victory in the 1980/81 season meant a home quarter-final tie vs Tottenham Hotspur. The Shed was heaving and with us being the Second Division side and shorn of our large rock of a defender Micky Droy, we were underdogs. Just before half-time, Mickey Fillery scored one of the finest direct free kicks seen at the North Stand end. The Shed erupted in a mass sea of elated fans parched of success for too long. Half-time was spent celebrating that goal and the atmosphere grew more intense anticipating more of the same in the second-half. It was, as so often in those days not to be. Chelsea were undone by a heady mixture of the likes of Steve Archibald, Osvaldo Ardiles and ultimately by Glenn Hoddle and Micky Hazard, the latter two of course to end up in blue in their later careers. The Shed had one last shout as Alan Mayes scored a consolation. The celebrations however were somewhat muted compared to earlier.

It is easy to say those were the days. The reality is that it was a ground well past its sell by date and even dangerous in parts. The crumbling terraces, the inadequate entrances... and yet speak to anyone of that era and it holds a magical status reminding us of our youth and of days that were truly carefree.

Modernisation has since then largely removed any trace of the old ground I grew up with barring the East Stand. The reality of the disasters in Glasgow, Bradford and Sheffield, did, quite rightly, force change. Our history is not now defined by Peter Osgood, Charlie Cooke and Alan Hudson but also by the likes of John Terry, Frank Lampard and Didier Drogba. I would not trade any of our recent adventures at home and abroad for the old days, but that does not stop me riding the crest of a wave of nostalgia and thinking of a bygone era as I enter Stamford Bridge through the Bovril Gate and climb the main steps to The Shed to be greeted by the sight of our stadium. My memories will live with me forever. "White wall 'til I die", anyone?

Charles Rose is a former Chairman and Executive Director of Chelsea Pitch Owners PLC. He writes a monthly column for the 'cfcuk' fanzine and can be found on Twitter @bedframble

THE NOSE KNOWS
Walter Otton

A tube train door groaning open; patter of gleeful feet and excited chatter; up the Fulham Broadway steps – wooden stairs underfoot; South West London air; dodging police horse manure; onions frying; a holler from a hamburger seller; a brown-haired man making pleas through a megaphone about Christ and the end of the world; I move to the left and quickly buy the new Chelsea Independent; scent of fresh fanzine print; I move forward looking at the bodies gathered outside Rosie's pub; right hand in pocket my thumb and forefinger stroke my plastic membership card; I pass a crumpled five pound note and two gold pound coins through the gap in the booth; an unlit dog end moves up and down in time with the click of the turnstile; the team are out on the pitch – I can't see them yet, I just know from the voices filtering down; cocking my ear like a dog listening for his master I hear a groaning and muttering about the substitutes; squeezing between a group of men that are moving too slowly for me I smell booze on their breath and I imagine a bar top and a line of ales, a pool cue and green felt, darts in the corner and coins feeding a juke box; still two years until I'm eighteen, mind.

    I bound up the concrete steps; (looking back I wish I had taken my time but I always ran up them); anticipation building in the air; at least half-hour 'til kick-off; there they are – the Chelsea players in Royal Blue stretching and passing, going through their warm ups – I move towards the middle of The Shed, I look out for Tall Paul (he's usually with his cousins) – I pat my front right jean pocket feeling the outline my membership card – now I'm reassured it's safe; I pat my front left jean pocket and pull out a battered pack of ten cigarettes – I've saved three as usual – discipline and budgeting – I lean back against the crash barrier, screw a pale orange filter between my lips, my prized Clipper lighter sparks up, I inhale and both hear and feel the tobacco burn; I carefully replace the lighter to the pack then the pack back to my pocket; I produce the fanzine from my back left jeans pocket; I study the away fans filtering in and wonder how many they'll being and how many fans we'll have; I look at the sky-line – might rain later. I look from the East Stand to the benches, to the West, to the terracing either side of me and in front of me and behind me the coppers loom tall in their box earning money to watch football; I haven't got the change for a hot chocolate or a Bovril – returning the cigarette to my lips I open up the fanzine.

    In early 2020, the 'Harvard Gazette' (the newspaper based out of Harvard University in Massachusetts), printed an article looking at how scent, emotion and memory are intertwined – and exploited. I read the article several times, mainly because it's something that has particularly intrigued me, but also because I wanted to explore how football markets itself as a product to exploit me as a customer. Once I was in the supermarket looking redundantly at a shelf of food when a lady walked past me wearing the same perfume as an old girlfriend who broke my heart at least ten years before. I hadn't smelt this scent for a decade – it took me to a place I didn't want to go to where rejection and brokenness once ruled the roost. It took me the rest of the day to shake it off – eventually the scent lingered no more. It dispersed and I pushed things forward. Another time when I was near the beach on a windy day, a kid walked past me with his hand in a bag of chips. As he shovelled fat greasy chips in his gob the hit of salt and vinegar blasted me back to a time on holiday with my family when I was doing exactly the same thing balanced on a breaker, when a huge gust of wind blew my eight-year-old frame up and away. In that moment I could feel the crunch of shingle in my face as I landed head first on the pebbles; I could taste a mouthful full of sand on my tongue and could see a cone of chips scattered towards the oncoming waves as my Dad and sister laughed and my Mum picked me up and brushed me down.

In 1913, French author Marcel Proust wrote a line in his book that became such a famous passage in literature (in football terms, think of the Makelele role) that it had its own name: The Proustian moment. He essentially wrote about carrying a spoonful of tea to his lips 'in which I had let soften a bit of madeleine. But at the very instant when the mouthful of tea mixed with cake crumbs touched my palate, I quivered, attentive to the extraordinary thing that was happening inside me.' The Harvard article goes onto say that an OLFACTORY BRANDING SPECIALIST (yes, you read that correctly) explained it was the nose that really was at work. The nose knows. Smell and memory are so closely linked because of the brain's anatomy. Smells are essentially handled by the olfactory bulb (at the front of the brain) that sends information to the body's central command for further processing! Odours take a direct route to the limbic system – the regions related to emotion and memory. When I first read those words 'limbic system' it made me think of limbs, goal celebrations, the euphoria of release when a goal goes in, humans hugging and falling over each other, the connection of celebration and skin and smell and the brain logging that as a memory and the addict in us wanting that to be reproduced – and don't the Premier League brand and the Chelsea Football Club marketing kings know it.

Dawn Goldworm is a woman that knows that aroma is big business. I read that Hotels often pump signature scents into rooms and lobbies. This made me think of a library – the stillness, the focus, the pages, the quiet, long tables to work at. And then there is the sportswear giant Nike. According to the Goldworm, Nike has a signature scent inspired by such things as '.... *the smell of a rubber basketball sneaker as it scrapes across the court and a soccer cleat in grass and dirt. The goal is to create immediate and memorable connections between brands and consumers.'* She has certainly done her homework. Smell is the only fully developed sense that a foetus has in the womb. She explained that people tend to smell in COLOUR.

The muddy grass on an away football pitch (for example Selhurst Park) in the winter can take me to the dirt in the grass of my early childhood outside my Granny's council flat. I can catch the tangy yellow marzipan from a Battenberg cake on my tongue, I see proper butter in ham sandwiches with the crusts sliced off and discarded, the bread cut in little triangles. Granddad is opening a can of Coke for me, the fizz tickling my nostrils, I watch him splitting the foil with a thumb nail down a two-finger KitKat – then I'm out and down the stairs playing football on the grass, practicing kick-ups, dribbling and commentating under my breath – putting my hand in my pocket and patting the mass of Panini stickers hoping the boys from the other flats come down and play football and swap stickers.

A dazzling sunset with pinks and purples and blues and oranges can transport me to Leicester away (April 2015) when our victory meant Chelsea only needed three more points to won the league. The sky was something else. Walking by water can take me to the wooden stands of Craven Cottage standing by the River Thames. I've got one eye on the River and one eye on the match – suddenly it's April 2013 and for thirteen minutes the away end stamped their feet and hollered, *'We are the Champions! Champions of Europe!'* We all have our Proustian moments, and there'll be with us until the day we die. Blue is the colour. Our senses are intertwined. As Peter Kenyon once perfectly put to us (in a business sense) that we had to renew our memberships because IT'S IN THE BLOOD. I renewed with gritted teeth because I knew he had cornered me as a consumer. Our Proustian moments are packaged and sold back to us at price. Live generously, keep the peace and keep smelling. May the aroma you leave behind you be a legacy full of kindness, hope and courage. And what about that ghastly Singha beer they sell at the Bridge? Tastes so much better when you're drinking it on holiday, doesn't it?

With thanks to the concrete steps up to The Shed End terracing, the 'Harvard Gazette' and the wonderfully named Dawn Goldworm.

Walter Otton's evocative writing style has been described as C.S. Lewis colliding explosively with The Streets. A multi-published author and scribe for the 'cfcuk' fanzine, his most recent book 'Let The Celery Decide. A Chelsea Tale From Barcelona And Munich' is highly recommended. You can follow Walter on Twitter @WalterOtton

AWAYDAY BLUES
Richard Schaller

"It was the best of times, it was the worst of times." The opening line to Charles Dickens famous novel, 'A Tale Of Two Cities'. An apt one when following Chelsea, especially back in the days from 1974 onwards when performances and fortunes would roller coaster between great, good, bad and unbelievably bad. Relegation followed by promotion and again relegation by 1979.

I'd started going to the Bridge as a lad from 1968 at the start of that golden era under Dave Sexton culminating in winning the FA Cup in 1970 and the European Cup Winners' Cup in 1971. By the time Ken Shellito was sacked following his brief stint as manager after he took over the reins from Eddie McCreadie, the decline after promotion in 1977 went from worse to worse. A lower-half finish at the end of our first season back in Division One simply papered over the cracks and even by the end of 1978 the following season it was clear we would be heading back to Division Two. It was very clear. We were at times awful. Even a fight back against Bolton Wanderers at the Bridge earlier in the season in which Chelsea came back from 3-0 down to win 4-3 could only be seen as a get-out-of-jail performance.

Even in 1978, Blues fans turned up in droves when travelling. I went to all but one home game during that 1978/79 season but maybe only half-a-dozen away games, mostly London and the South because of my job. I worked in London and had digs in town too so even if the football was crap there were gigs and girlfriends. Things could have been a lot worse!

I'd often go to Chelsea with a mate Terry, (sadly no longer with us). He was a good laugh. I told him I fancied a road trip to an away game up north if he fancied it as well but he wasn't keen. However, I was getting friendly with a guy at work named Mike who was also Chelsea and he was up for it. So I marked the Middlesbrough game leading up to Christmas as the one to go to. There was however a significant problem to overcome. I didn't have a car. I never needed one living in London. When I mentioned my plans to another mate he said I could use his for that weekend. So I cheerfully went to pick it up in Barking. I didn't bother with insurance or to even check its road worthiness. I just got in and drove off. It was an old Ford Anglia. Very old. A mix of sky blue and rust. The smell of oil was noticeable and the passenger wiper was missing but it was good just to drive again.

We set off at about 6am on that Saturday morning. It was cold but the fuel tank was topped up and with our stuff put in the back off we went. I'd booked a bed and breakfast outside Middlesbrough by telephone so all was good. We drove up the A1 stopping off for a fry-up and a beer on the way. The A1 covered pretty much three-quarters of the journey until near Harrogate then there were a couple of A roads to Middlesbrough. It was all good for the first five hours or so of driving but then oil fumes started making us both queasy. I stopped and checked a very black-looking engine and decided to check the oil after the game. What didn't help matters was my companion Mike turning out to be as dull as ditch water. Jokes weren't hitting home and he didn't seem to want to chat as much as I'd expected. One subject we did talk about was the impending return of Peter Osgood and the news that Danny Blanchflower had been appointed as Chelsea's new gaffer. I think he was Northern Ireland manager just before but other than that it was a huge surprise. But Ossie was back and we would hope he'd make his return debut at Ayresome Park where we were heading to.

Middlesbrough is built-up so we wanted to park fairly close to the ground but ended up getting lost so we parked anywhere, which wasn't that far in the end but still far enough. It was probably going to be difficult trying to find our way through terraced streets that all looked exactly the same, but no matter, we set off walking to the ground. As we did so, I looked back at the car and noticed the two front hubcaps were missing. They must have each detached themselves on the way.

We got to the ground about 1.30pm and already Chelsea fans were there in numbers. We looked for the away supporters section and as we did so it was obvious that a huge contingent of Blues fans were heading the opposite way towards the Holgate End, Boro's home end! There was a narrow walkway behind the Holgate End. I suggested we venture down it to get to the away section on the other side. Wrong move. A handful of Boro boys were walking towards us not looking friendly at all and sadly not colour blind either as they noticed Mike's blue and white scarf. I suppose today they'd shout 'Rent Boys' to us but they shouted something different then that I couldn't understand other than the supposition that we were some soft species from the South. They started towards us which made my heart pound. Mike ran off. Well pal I don't think you and me will be mates for long. I don't know why I froze but I did. Haven't a clue why? Rabbit in headlamps stuff I suppose. I've been pummelled before so I began to reassure myself that eventually you will go numb. Just then (like the cavalry) a mob of Chelsea fans appeared who were also not colour blind and went straight for the Boro mob. This narrow walkway became a small battlefield. Like the fog of war I had to fend off one Chelsea fan who took a swipe at me before I quickly told him in my London accent I was Chelsea!

Getting away I met up with Mike again and joked if we ended up in the trenches together I'd still be on my own. He didn't seem to get it. When we eventually got inside the ground we could see Chelsea fans battling away in the Holgate End before the game. I shook my head in admiration. Chelsea fans around me then started to sing 'Osgood, Osgood', as the teams ran out. It was freezing and I didn't feel at all well. Neither did Mike. The game was not going to make us feel any better.

Chelsea got off to a great start when Osgood headed in to put us a goal up. He ran to us in the corner with his fists raised. We sang his name again this time to let everyone know that the great man was back and continued with '1-0, 1-0', to the tune of 'Amazing Grace'. That's about as good as it got football-wise. Boro hit back almost immediately and before we knew it we were 3-1 down. So our delight was very brief before normal service was resumed and our defence crumbled once again. Delight from the Boro fans who by now were in full control of the Holgate End.

There was no respite in the second-half sadly and as a plainly tired Osgood was replaced by Clive Walker, Boro's Micky Burns and the brilliant Terry Cochrane ripped us apart further. The former netting four times in the match. We kept losing the ball they kept moving it up to our goal to score. You know the picture. A young hard-working Johnny Bumstead pulled a goal back but when the final whistle went with scoreboard displaying Boro 7 Chelsea 2 I couldn't wait to get out of the ground. Seeing so many dire performances from us previously there was no shock just a numbness to it all. I was still feeling very nausea as was Mike and thought maybe we'd either eaten something dodgy on the way or more likely the oil fumes from the car on the way up had started the process of gradually poisoning us both.

We walked back to the car. The bed and breakfast was a pub called The Anchor Inn in Guisborough several miles away. I checked the oil first which was thankfully still in the engine. Halfway there, the fumes proved too much and we both got out to vomit. Did we feel better? Not much. We got to the pub and what was turning out to be anything other than a memorable weekend started to improve as the Anchor was a very decent establishment. After we booked in, I suggested maybe a beer and then a bite of pub food. Mike went out and vomited again. He wasn't a bundle of fun but then with both of us feeling unwell I probably wasn't either. That said, the whole point of this road trip away day weekend was to have a right laugh.

We downed a decent cooked breakfast the following morning and set off home feeling better. When I started the engine a huge billow of black smoke left the exhaust before we moved off. I'm not a car mechanic but it was obvious this old girl was struggling. The oil smell was stronger and the queasiness returned. We talked a bit about Chelsea but as we did so it dawned on me that the car was losing power as we drove along the edge of the Yorkshire Moors towards Harrogate. When we reached Thirsk the car's power was so sluggish I thought at this rate we'd be lucky to get back to London before the end of the week. Eventually, we weren't going anywhere as the engine suddenly juddered and the oil fumes became even stronger before the car finally gave up with more black smoke coming from the exhaust and now also coming from under the bonnet. When I opened it the engine looked like it had been coated in thick black gloss paint. It was oil. Everywhere. And a burning smell too. The engine was kaput!

I telephoned (from a box) a local mechanic who charged me £10 to come and have a look and tell me the bloody obvious and then a further £25 to tow it away to the breakers yard. A fair bit of dosh back then. I telephoned my mate who'd lent me the car who said not to worry as being such an old motor I'd probably done him a favour. "That's ok mate it's a pleasure," I replied. He laughed. I realised I'd probably been tucked up.

And so it came to pass that this so-called road trip ended up with me and Fun Mike spending the next few hours getting back to London by train and I eventually got back to my digs late on Sunday night. At work the following morning, my colleagues were laughing at the Chelsea result and asked how the weekend went. I suggested they asked my travelling companion Fun Mike when he got in.

Supremely talented artist Richard provided the wonderful illustrations for the front and back cover of this book and has had his work featured in many publications including 'The Jam: The start to '77' and 'Come Along And Sing This Song: Chelsea 1983-1984'. You can follow him on Twitter @richschaller54

BLUE PYJAMAS AND RED SQUARE
Iain Rodger

"The past is a foreign country; they do things differently there".

That's what L.P. Hartley wrote in his 1953 novel, 'The Go-Between'. How we understand the past and how we sift and choose our memories is a life-long activity. Moments of seemingly great importance can fade, inconsequential details often remain. Our settled view of our past, our assumptions as to what it meant are never constants. It changes according to time, place and our own private logic.

Who knew that a pair of pyjamas and a car journey in 1966 would change my life forever? And who knew the link it would have with Red Square, Moscow in 2008?

The story begins at Christmas 1965. Father Christmas had given this particular 8-year-old the only present he wanted; The 'Charles Buchan Football Annual'. The first colour football annual to be published in the UK. Pictures of individual players, team photographs, lists of grounds. In colour! That was my idea of fun. I'd devour every word. I'd stare at every page for what seemed like hours on end. Santa always came up with the best presents.

The blue pyjamas with a football crest on them that my parents bought me were initially far less exciting of course. Until, while wearing them, reading my Annual, I turned the page and saw a team also wearing blue. The shirt had a white collar, white shorts, black socks with blue and white tops. I looked at that shirt, looked at my blue pyjamas and told my Dad, "That's Chelsea, Dad. Can I support Chelsea?"

It's usually geography or family affiliation that bestows on you the team you support. As has often been said, you don't choose your football team, it's chosen for you. Just not usually by the colour of your pyjamas.

Was I born in London and did my Dad support Chelsea? No and no. I was born in Glasgow and my Dad was a regular attender of Partick Thistle games ("Firhill for thrills", I can still hear him say). He very sensibly decided, the family having moved to Redhill in Surrey when I was a toddler, that he wouldn't submit me to that particular torture. He simply nodded and said yes. I was a Chelsea fan by Boxing Day.

My next question was clear and immediate; "When can I go and watch Chelsea play, Dad? They play at Stamford Bridge. Do you know where that is?" If I asked him once, I must have asked him a hundred times. But apparently I was too young and would have to wait until I went to Big School. Which was of course a lifetime away for this particular 8-year-old.

As 1965 clicked over into 1966, one January Saturday morning my Dad said we were off to London for the day to do a bit of sight-seeing. I got into the back seat of our Ford Anglia and we headed off. We had only gone about seven miles when we stopped in Banstead where my Dad told me we were picking up a friend of his en route. "It's that house there, son. Just go and knock on the door and tell him we're here".

I knocked on the door. It opened. And there was Peter Bonetti looking down at me. "You must be Iain. Are you going to the match today?" Answer came there none. Just a wide-eyed, jaw-dropping silence. "We'd better get going then", he said.

We left our car, got into his and set off for Stamford Bridge. Dad in the passenger seat, me in the back. I'd like to be able to tell you I remember the conversation well but I don't. Dumbstruck, the journey passed in a blur. I'm sure Peter would have been generous enough to ask me some questions. I'm even more sure my answers would have been monosyllabic.

It's possible I asked him who we were playing. I loved being able to say "we". He told me Spurs. I wasn't sure if that was the same team as Tottenham Hotspur who I'd seen in my Annual but I suspected it might be. A mere 10 miles on and I was at Stamford Bridge for the first time. Peter drove straight in past the ticket office and parked beside the ivy-clad main office. That's where the hotel is now, just beside the Away entrance to The Shed.

When we got out of the car, (Peter Bonetti's car!), Peter offered his hand which I shook and he said, "Enjoy the match, kid!" We walked to our seats in the East Stand. "I didn't know you knew Peter Bonetti, Dad?!" Turned out my Dad didn't. It was all arranged by a friend of his, a fellow Scot, who was a neighbour of Peter's in Banstead.

I can remember anything of the match itself. I just remember the green of the pitch, the noise of the songs, people standing up and shouting. It was utterly intoxicating. The record shows that there were 48,529 spectators that day. Inevitably, some others there for the first time too, I suppose. The score? Well, my diary for that day (which I still have) says, "Went to my first Chelsea game. Chelsea beat Spurs 2-1. Skill!" How could I not be a Chelsea fan after that introduction?

The record also shows that I saw for the first time that day, many of the players who would go on to win Chelsea's first FA Cup some four years later. Names that still echo through the years as Chelsea greats; Harris, McCreadie, Hollins, Hinton, Osgood and of course Bonetti, my personal chauffeur. Bobby Tambling, who would go on to score more goals for Chelsea than any other player before Frank came along, also played that day. There were even a couple of players in our team who would go on to manage Spurs and Arsenal in Terry Venables and George 'Stroller' Graham. The latter, along with Peter Osgood, scored our two goals that day.

After the match, we got the train to Banstead and picked up the car. I told my Mum every detail when we got home. And repeated those details every day for months, especially to my schoolmates. It certainly did my school cred no harm at all.

What has any of this got to do with Red Square, Moscow some 42-years later? Well, it was of course our first Champions League Final. Across the Square before the match, there was Peter Bonetti with friends. I went over to him and said, "Peter, you're the reason I'm here today". Unsurprisingly, he had no memory of the lift he'd given me that day but certainly remembered his house in Banstead that we'd set out from. We chatted for a few minutes, true gentleman that he was.

He passed away in 2020. I'm delighted we have a banner very close to where I sit in The Shed that pays tribute to The Cat. And if you ever catch me gazing at it with a far-away look, you'll know I'm not really there. I'm 8-years-old and it's January 1966.

Iain Rodger is a Chelsea season ticket holder and Chelsea Pitch Owners shareholder. He writes a popular column for the 'cfcuk' fanzine entitled 'Iain Rodger's Media Mash-Up'. You can follow Iain on Twitter @IainRodger1

STAND UP, SIT DOWN
Jonathan Kydd

Saturday, February 3, 2007. I was sitting just in front of the horizontal gangway at The Valley, home of Charlton Athletic, in the away supporters' end. I mean by this that the away area seats are accessed by a 'path' that runs the length of the stand about halfway up. It divides the two sections of seating and I was at the lip of the first tier. I could therefore see the whole of the pitch without having to stand up. There was no one in front of me other than red be-bibbed security staff with their walky-talkies and they were standing on the path below me and not obstructing my view as I was several feet above them. In front of me, about seven-yards away, were the disabled seats to which the wheelchairs obviously had access as they could just wheel themselves along the path to these areas. In front of them was the other bank of seats populated by Chelsea fans all keen to stand up for the whole of the match if they could.

I've never quite got my head round this 'standing up'. Why pay £40 for a seat and then not sit in it? For a start off I'm only little and can't see very well over people's heads standing up. There's a theory that you can't sing well whilst sitting and this is why the supporters stand so they can get into the physical aspect of belting out a 'Blue Flag' or a 'Carefree'. But I rather like just taking the strain off my pins and supporting cerebrally rather than externally. I'll join in 'One Man Went To Mow' a bit. But not manically. I'll say, "Come on Chels" with the best. I'll gargle a 'You Are My Chelsea' at low volume. I'll hum a 'Zigger Zagger'. I'll whisper a 'Molly Malone' or 'We Will Follow The Chelsea'. And I'll whistle along to 'Chelsea, Chelsea, Chelsea, Chelsea' to the tune of 'Amazing Grace'.

As I say, I have a gap in front of me so can sit without the game being obstructed. To my right and below, the bank of Chelsea fans have decided that standing is the order of the day and they're all up. Next to me a sweaty, nastily-sweet smelling man is twitching to stand and sing to everything. Even he can see the futility of standing when there's no one in front of you but the bank to our right are all up despite the urging of the stewards to get them to sit. Frank Lampard scores for Chelsea in the 18th minute and the stewards give up. A man in a wheelchair is incandescent. "Get em to sit down. I can't see," he shouts. He tries a canny trick and elevates his chair which has a sort of forklift truck device in it which raises his chair up a few feet. But this is no good. He gives up and sinks back in his chair and peers between the upright bodies. His pal next to him in his chair, tries reasoning with his fellow Chelsea fans who stare at him blankly and carry on standing. Because to be fair if they were to sit down they wouldn't be able to see themselves. He rather peculiarly gets out of his chair and 'Little Britain-like', stands beside it to watch the game. To my left the disabled viewers have instigated a revolt and have shamed the standees to sit, allowing them a clear view.

All good, however in the second-half the situation changes. Chelsea rather dully decide to defend their 1-0 lead. Didier Drogba occupies the left-wing and not to put too fine a word to it 'nancies about'. Michael Ballack does an impression of an uninterested pouting ballerina and Charlton come back into it and almost score twice. Thanks to the competence of Petr Cech they don't but it's a close thing. Chelsea are feeble. The crowd start cat-calling. People stand up out of boredom. You think it'd be the other way round, but no. They're encouraged commendably to, 'stand up for the Che-el-sea' by the men attempting to get the team to play better through noise and crowd support. The din level goes up for a bit while the competence level goes down. The irritation level goes up as well. To the left a bloke stands up in front of another bloke sitting in a 'Multi-Coloured Swap Shop' of a wheelchair with Chelsea badges on the wheels. "Could you sit down mate? I can't see," asks the disabled fellow. "No mate! F*ck off!" replies the delightfully charming man whose face I notice has sunken features. I heard it all. The man in the CFC decorated wheelchair decides to punch him in the face and does so rather expertly. The punched man is left with a dilemma. He can't really fight the disabled guy because he'd look dreadful in the eyes of his fellow supporters so he finds an excuse to punch the man next to him who looked as if he'd told him off for telling the disabled guy to f*ck off! A third man enters the fray for no apparent reason I can see. A flurry of punches causes all three to leave their seats and tumble down the gangway where others join in in a very ad hoc manner. It's almost as if the attitude is one of, "Oh look! People fighting. I might as well join in". The stewards don't intervene. They whisper into their walkie-talkies and an elite Swat-style squad in red bibs trot in and attempt to rein in the 'trouble', snatching people from the melee and frogmarching them away. A bloke who's been for a wee and had nothing at all to do with anything looms nearby and is captured and strong-armed off despite legitimate protestations. Near the entrance to the stand some supporters on a level with me jump down expertly and throw punches at the stewards just because they can. The smelly man to my right is hoping the incident escalates so he can pitch in. He exhibits his desire for involvement by twitching and flexing and leaning over me to get a better view.

Meanwhile, on the pitch, Chelsea are frightful. I have to admit that what is happening in the stand is much more interesting than the game taking place, but even this quietens down as everyone squeakily endures the prospect of The Blues, so dominant in the first-half that their opponents kept ineptly giving the ball away like frightened teenagers, possibly losing. The focus shifts from boredom to dreadful anxiety. No one wants to fight now. They want the team to fight. Luckily, Salomon 'hasn't got a' Kalou and the boy badly chasing a balloon that is Shaun Wright-Philips come off the subs benched and attack a bit more causing Charlton to once again reveal themselves as keen to give the ball away and so 90-minutes are reached without disaster.

Jonathan Kydd is a renown voiceover artist and actor. He co-presents the Chelsea Football Fancast and in 2021 published the memoirs of his late father, the actor Sam Kydd. You can follow JK on Twitter @Jonathankydd

THE ONLY TEAM IN LONDON (TWICE)
Alexandra Churchill

I watched the Moscow final in a pub in Sutton. I wanted to lay out the Manc standing next to me in all his smug glory and by the end of it I wanted to lay out Didier Drogba too. At that point I'd convinced myself that didn't care about the Champions League. I 100% didn't want to go through that again. And yet like a mug, because who can resist it, really, I spent the next four years wishing and praying my way through our European adventures in the hope that one day, preferably before any of the other London clubs, we might win it.

I'd been blasé about Munich all week. Having watched us spin it against Napoli in what might be the best atmosphere I remember at the Bridge, and having royally screwed Barca in their own backyard, I'd been telling everyone it was written in the stars. It would just be cruel; it would be a colossal disappointment worse than the third Godfather film if we'd have ended this story with anything other than the trophy. All day long we'd been faced with a smuggery about the city on the face of their contingent. They seemed to regard it as a foregone conclusion, which wound me right up. They'd even had t-shirts made. Their city, their stadium, their trophy. Bugger that! Throughout the course of the day some wise German who didn't like them one bit had also told me that Bayern were basically the Man United of the Bundesliga, bussing in plastics and glory-hunters from the length and breadth of the country, which made me a little less pragmatic about not overcoming the odds. Now, as I walked up to the ground and realised it was their back yard I came face-to-face with the ugliest kid you can imagine, decked out in Bayern gear and gurning at us, telling us we were going to get battered. Short of punting him, which, which might have been frowned upon, we were going to have to batter them now. Consider me well and truly fired up.

I have very few memories of the 90-minutes, other than that, very unusually for me when they scored with about five minutes to go, I did not crap my pants. I remember thinking: "nah, this isn't done yet." Normally I'd have been clawing my eyes out and having a meltdown. I remember <u>knowing</u> that Drogba was going to score that equaliser without any doubt whatsoever. I remember that Gary Cahill and David Luiz were absolutely buggered during extra time, and that Paulo Ferreira was fully ready to go, bouncing up and down waiting to run on when one of them inevitably collapsed. Both of them had dud hamstrings and neither would have been on the pitch had it not been a final.

AN ANTHOLOGY OF STORIES AND ARTICLES ABOUT CHELSEA FC

You basically witnessed every possible human emotion during the penalty shoot out. People have a routine. My friend Danielle's routine was to run and hide behind a burger van and periodically peep out every time one group of fans cheered. Fully-grown men were using each other as human shields and hiding behind flags. And usually I am the biggest wuss going, but by the time I figured out what Chelsea had done, that they had lined Drogba up to take number five, I was adamant that we were going to win it. I turned to my football bro and said, "his ego isn't going to let him miss." I have more memories of the celebrations than anything. Said football bro suddenly had his shirt off and wrapped round his head. He was wearing a flag as a skirt and now looked like the worlds creepiest belly dancer. Branislav Ivanovic mounted the crossbar and nearly broke it. And we'd be lying if we said that the fact that we managed to screw Spurs out of the Champions League didn't make it even better. I remember saying: "I'd love to see Harry Redknapp's face right now." As if by magic, there it was on the big screen and we were all pointing and laughing. Funnily enough, Drogba's penalty is now harder to watch 10 years later because I'm convinced he's going to miss!

You'd be forgiven for thinking that it could never quite be as epic second time around, but in its way, it was. Fast-forward nine years to a season when we never, really, should have been anywhere near the final on paper. Our season had looked dire at the turn of the year. And once again, looking at the opposition, were we ridiculous to believe that we might turn Pep Guardiola over? The world had been through a pandemic and life had changed beyond all recognition. We'd been locked up, some of our nearest and dearest fans were gone, and at this point we were all done. And then suddenly we were on a plane to Porto. The sun was shining and we were doing a European away. It was surreal. Half the seats were taped off, there were 1001 hoops to jump through but it felt like a reward for a year of misery.

I've got even less recollections of the game in Porto than I do of Munich. What I do remember is the goal, and feeling marginally guilty about facing all the Manchester City fans in our hotel who had wanted this so, so badly. For about five seconds. But more than anything, I remember that in the space between the two finals, the pandemic had claimed my football "dad," and that I watched this game with someone else who had lost the nearest thing to a grandmother he has, with whom he went home and away. When the final whistle went, before we started celebrating there were a few tears for the people who hadn't made it through to the other side of this thing with us.

I like that Frank Lampard was in our thoughts that night in Porto after it hadn't worked out with him in charge at Stamford Bridge. Ask me what my favourite Champions League moment is and it's neither of the winning finals, it's actually more to do with Super Frank. Let me take you back to 2009, and firstly a road trip to the land of Scouse for the first leg of a quarter-final tie with Liverpool. It started terribly. Before Chelsea shelled out a fortune for Fernando Torres and broke their fanbase, the then darling of the Kop put The Reds ahead after six minutes. I was convinced that we were going to take a complete pasting however it soon turned into one of the best awaydays ever thanks to Two-Goal-Branislav-Ivanovic who shut the Scousers right up and then Drogba made it 1-3. "**** your history, we're going to Rome." I don't think I slept until the following night I was so high on demolishing them.

"Don't worry about a thing" Chelsea. Just keep your sh*t together in the second leg at the Stamford Bridge and "every little thing is gonna be all right". As if we were ever going to be able to do that. I do remember that in the first half-hour all of the glory at theirs was reversed and when Liverpool went 2-0 up we were bricking it. Unfortunately, then, someone behind us lit possibly the most pungent spliff I've ever sniffed in my life and the whole night became a rampant, polarised blur that shot between agony and jubilation as the aggregate score kept changing. Walking out of the Bridge, I could not have told you what order the goals came in or whether we'd come out on top. I later found out, when I was wandering round a 24-hour Tesco with the munchies singing "Blue is the Colour" at 2:00am and waving a flag that the game had finished 4-4 and Super Frank had scored a brace sealing the qualification deal (7-5 on aggregate) with a last-minute goal.

The less said about how that Champions League campaign ended, the better!

Alex Churchill is a royal and military historian, multi-published author and Chelsea home and away season ticket holder. You can follow her on Twitter @churchill_alex

THANK YOU, MR MEEHAN
Mark Worrall

I hope you have enjoyed reading this anthology of short stories and articles. If you purchased this book you have helped a very worthy cause. Homelessness, food insecurity and associated mental health issues have accelerated in the wake of the Covid-19 pandemic meaning local government authorities that were already under pressure are now seriously struggling to cope. This is why initiatives such as the 'Big Stamford Bridge Sleep Out' are so vitally important; not only to raise funds to assist people living in crisis but also to increase awareness of problems that should not exist in modern society and motivate everyone to make a positive difference.

As a project, editing 'Tales From The Shed' highlighted for me the wealth of writing talent, creativity, generosity, compassion and community spirit that exists among Chelsea supporters. It's a shame this goodwill is widely overlooked by the media who only seem truly energised when crisis, conflict or controversy shroud Stamford Bridge.

From a personal perspective, writing and publishing and encouraging others to write and get published has proved to be my salvation from bouts of more-often-than-not self-inflicted misery, anxiety and depression. I'll share my story now about how my writing journey started and developed in the hope that it will encourage troubled souls to seek help and stimulate readers to reach out more often to friends and acquaintances who have dropped off the radar and/or maybe going through a tough time.

Sunday, January 12, 1992

5am. I wasn't asleep. I hadn't been asleep, and I had no intentions of trying to sleep. The previous day, Chelsea 2 Tottenham Hotspur 0, had been one long buzz and when I'd got home, shortly before 2am, I'd decided to prolong the high by continuing to get bang on it. Vodka, half an ecstasy tablet I'd found down the back of the sofa on Friday night, vodka, the remnants of the day's packet of cocaine, vodka, amyl nitrate, vodka, cannabis, vodka, vodka, vodka. By 3am I was pouring vodka onto a teaspoon and snorting it. I don't recommend trying this, but in my pursuit of a higher high it seemed like a good idea.

With the lights dimmed low, I danced around my living room throwing shadow shapes against the wall. I had one tune on endless repeat 'Unfinished Sympathy' by Massive Attack. I always had one tune on endless repeat when I partied solo which I seemed to be doing with increasing frequency. My (soon-to-be-ex) wife wouldn't have been impressed but she'd gone to stay at her mother's for the weekend (again). I knew we were having problems (all of them down to my selfish addiction to getting high... higher than everyone else) that needed addressing, but right now my only concern was the fact I'd run out of booze and drugs; a schoolboy error that I couldn't remedy as I wasn't well-connected enough (yet). There were a couple of all-night dance clubs I thought about heading to where I might get 'served' but outside a Baltic gale was howling and the rain accompanying it was lashing down torrentially. Plus, what if the doormen refused me entry... or allowed me in and then threw me out?

Paranoia took hold! I contemplated getting a rental in just for some company and telephoned a local escort agency, but I was so far off my head I couldn't string two sentences together and the receptionist hung up on me! I was stuck. I'd just have to tough out the come down and inevitable vampire hangover. I picked up a copy of the 'Chelsea Independent' fanzine I'd bought before the Spurs game and read it cover-to-cover and then I read it again. Maybe I should write an article for the fanzine, that would help pass the time. Good idea! I lit a cigarette, sat down at the kitchen table and put biro to paper.

The previous weekend I'd gone up to Hull to watch Chelsea play an FA Cup game. It was a cracking day out and the Blues had won 2-0 so I decided to write about that. I wrote three versions of the article. As I'd read the back the first version, I recalled more about the day and the game and so wrote a second version and then a third. Eventually I gave up at 7am when the effects of the gear had worn off sufficiently for me go to bed. What I learned later when my equilibrium returned and I read those three articles again stood me in good stead for the future. Don't try and write under the influence of drugs as the resultant stream of altered-state-of-consciousness will be incoherent, rambling nonsense. I re-wrote the article for a fourth time, titled it 'To Hull And Back' and sent it off to the editor of the fanzine, a gentleman I didn't know at that time by the name of Mark Meehan who published it in the next edition. I thought this was great and my friends I went to games with really enjoyed reliving our adventure and told me I should write more; however instead of pursuing my newly found creative alternative to self-destruction I shelved it in favour of increased excesses which culminated in divorce which in turn presented me with an outstanding opportunity to go completely off the rails... which I embraced compulsively!

Monday, October 23, 1999

7am. "You think that stuff makes you invincible." I laughed at my latest girlfriend's words as she shook her head and opened the door to leave the house and go to work. She was right. I watched as a double dose of

Berocca tablets fizzed in a pint of sparkling water turning it orange as they dissolved. I picked up the glass, necked the drink down in one and shook my head vigorously as the carbon dioxide bubbles erupted inside me. Still water and one tablet would have sufficed, but I believed the sparkling variety and a double-drop would turbo-charge the speed at which the Vitamin C equivalent of consuming five times my body weight in oranges coursed around my body. My immune system would be boosted to such an extent that I would be invincible! "Invincible!" I shouted after my girlfriend as she slammed the door shut behind her.

Five minutes later, the doorbell rang. It wasn't my girlfriend returning, it was a taxi driver. The time had arrived for me to go to go Heathrow to board a flight to Milan (Chelsea were playing AC Milan in a Champions League match the following day). It didn't matter that I hadn't been to sleep since Friday. Three hours kip that night had been my sole concession to sensibility ahead of a what I knew would be a crazy few days which had started at 9am on Saturday morning with a cheeky line of sparkle before heading to Stamford Bridge to watch Chelsea v Arsenal.

I can't remember why we'd decided to watch this game from the West Stand which was undergoing redevelopment and currently comprised of one tier and no roof, or why we weren't suitably attired for the wet weather that surely must have been forecast, but when the ever-darkening clouds swirling above our heads with a murky malevolence opened up and spewed forth a biblical deluge that would have been enough to convince Noah to board his animals on his ark it felt like a bad idea. As I watched my matchday programme rapidly disintegrate to mush (I never bought one again), I was grateful that I had my stash of gear for the day securely wrapped up in clingfilm and concealed in a small, waterproof, polythene zip lock bag.

On the pitch it was classic Chelsea, and by that I mean the snatching defeat from the jaws of victory version of Chelsea that has bedevilled the Club since it was founded in 1905. Glorious unpredictability of the horrible kind. We were singing in the rain in the 38th minute when "Tore, Tore Andre Flo" headed home a smart Dan Petrescu cross and then on 52 minutes it was "Dan, Dan Super Dan" who made it 2-0 getting his head to a pinpoint Graeme Le Saux cross. Someone started a conga, and everyone got up singing, "Let's all do the conga." The stewards weren't impressed, the Old Bill didn't care and some Arsenal fans started leaving (no surprise there). I took an ecstasy tablet to enhance my celebratory mood and just as I started coming up, Nwankwo Kanu pulled a goal back for the Gunners... it was the first goal Chelsea had conceded at the Bridge so far this season.

My head was spinning. Although I was as wet as an otter's pocket, my skin felt dry. I held my hands up and gazed at the tips of my fingers which had gone all wrinkly. It reminded me of being a kid and sitting in the bath too long. My mate Ugly John was next to me and started laughing so I gave him a hug and told him I loved him and then Kanu scored again. "Okay, okay, we'll take the draw." Into the last minute and I was absolutely flying!

"Ed De Goey, Oi!! Ed De Goey," I started singing for no apparent reason. Plenty joined in, but instead of taking inspiration from our support De Goey had a rush of blood to the head. Arsenal's man of the moment, Kanu, scampered through the puddles down to the by line with the ball seemingly welded to his feet, the Chelsea goalie lumbered out and made a despairing challenge and was rounded and beaten by a shot from the narrowest of angles. 2-0 had evolved into 2-3! What a shocker! I'd have to take more drugs to blot out the memory!

After leaving the Bridge we headed to a club on Fulham Broadway called the Leopard Lounge and made use of the hot air hand driers in the toilets to dry our clothes and ended up staying there until 3am (not just in the toilets) at which point it was all back to mine for the after-party which continued through Sunday.

Honestly, I thought I was having the best time it was possible to have. The hours and days flew over and the next thing I knew I was in the San Siro watching Dennis Wise score "a ******* great goal" that would soon be immortalised in song. When I got home on Wednesday evening I found a hastily scrawled note on the kitchen table from my (now-ex) girlfriend politely advising me that my reply to her angry "I think you love Chelsea more than me" text had been inappropriate. I checked my phone. "I love Tottenham more than you," I'd replied. Oh dear! I was inconsolable for as long as it took me to chop out a line of gear, pour myself a large vodka and call the escort agency.

Saturday, January 26, 2002

I'd been feeling a bit rough for several days. A pinching pain in my flank and dull ache in my lower back had both refused to respond to the usual over-the-counter pharmacy medicines and I was also passing blood when I went to the toilet. Not good, but these ailments weren't going to stop me going to the football! Chelsea v West Ham United, an FA Cup Fourth Round tie... it promised to be a cracker!

There was a new-to-me party drug on the scene called ketamine which I'd been told was principally used in hospital operating theatres to sedate patients ahead of surgery and manage pain. In a recreational scenario, taking ketamine was said to induce a dream-like, semi-hallucinogenic state. Brilliant! Just what I needed. I'd ordered some in along with the usual supplies. Ketamine did the trick and my pain vanished. I took so much on the morning of the game that if I'd been tied to a bench and hacksawed in half I wouldn't have felt a thing.

"Oh Jimmy, Jimmy. Jimmy, Jimmy, Jimmy Floyd Hasselbaink." In the 21st minute, Hasselbaink scored one of the most beautiful Chelsea goals I'd seen up to this point in my history of going to games and I'm not just saying this because I was on the gear though I did have flashbacks for a long time afterwards which might have enhanced this recollection. Having gained possession 40-yards-or-so out on the touchline the Dutch striker panicked the West Ham defence into backing off and then shimmied before clipping the ball deftly in what seemed to me to be a slow-motion-looping goal-bound arc. I stood up and looked on mesmerised as the ball sailed over the head of bemused Hammers keeper David James into the top corner of the net. Brilliant! Chelsea should have kicked on and made sure of victory, but instead they allowed the visitors back into the game and Frederic Kanoute equalised late on to send the tie to a replay.

After the game I went to the pub for a few drinks but around 7pm the pain in my abdomen returned. I was out of ketamine so I decided to get a taxi home, I'd smoke some weed that would sort me out. I could get through Sunday and if I was still feeling rough on Monday I'd go to the doctors.

Things didn't go to plan! By 11pm I was on my knees on my kitchen floor howling in pain. It felt as if I was being stabbed in my bladder with a red-hot poker. Having given up on conventional relationships after the Milan incident I was living on my own so had no one on-hand to help me in my hour of need. In my paranoid state-of-mind I'd already decided that calling 999 was a bad idea. What if the Ambulance crew clocked I was on gear and informed the Old Bill and they turned up and gave my drum a spin? My house was an Aladdin's Cave of nefarious illegality, the local constabulary would find enough merchandise to stick some charge or other on me and then Human Resources at work would find out and things would really come on top. I called a mate who came round and drove me to the Accident and Emergency department at Epsom General Hospital. By now I was on the verge of passing out, the pain was so intense. I was seen immediately, and relief came swiftly in the form of morphine administered by a nurse who I recognised from the local house party scene. I swear she was smiling as she pushed the needle in.

Wednesday, 6 February, 2002

I spent over a week in hospital during which time I'd learnt that the primary cause of my pain was a collection of large kidney stones that had decided to block my urinary tracts. I'd had an operation to break them up and eventually been allowed home. In the general scheme of sinister medical issues, it wasn't that serious, I was lucky. The consultant who treated me suggested that if I wanted to avoid having stones form again, I needed to make certain 'lifestyle' changes and drink plenty of water to avoid becoming dehydrated. I thanked him for healing me and for the advice and vowed to give up drugs and booze and try to be a better person. I was 40-years-old and most of my friends had already settled down and started families, maybe the time had come for me to do the same.

I got home early in the afternoon and my thoughts soon turned to football and the replay of the Chelsea / West Ham FA Cup tie. I'd thought about going to Upton Park but I still had a stent inside me following my operation and this kept making me feel like I needed to go to the toilet which I was doing quite often anyway as I was following the consultant's advice to the letter and drinking more water than a fish! I idled away the hours tidying up, sorting my wardrobe out and reading and then at 10.35pm I settled down in front of my TV to watch 'Match of the Day' which was featuring extended highlights of the replay. I'd switched my mobile phone off to avoid getting score updates and messages from mates who'd gone to the game and was treated to an error-strewn goalfest which saw the Blues edge out the Hammers 3-2 thanks to a stoppage-time John Terry winner. Chelsea forced a corner. Graeme Le Saux pinged the ball into the penalty area, Steve Lomas headed it behind for another corner. Le Saux tried again. This time JT raced into the crowded penalty area, beat Tomas Repka to the ball and headed it in off the post. I leapt off the sofa and punched the air; as I did so my stent flexed and I winced in pain and sat down sharply. I imagined how lively it would be down Green Street after the game, no doubt I'd hear all about it from my mates the next day.

I went to bed and lay still in the darkness thinking about life and the fact that despite all the fun I'd been having how lonely I was and how horrible it was to be alone and in pain and then just as I dozed off to sleep I had a panic attack. I had no idea it was a panic attack as I'd never had one before. I awoke to a sense of unease creeping up on me and then simultaneously my heart started racing, I started sweating profusely and felt like I couldn't breathe or move. I was absolutely terrified and thought I was going to die.

Eventually, I'd grabbed my mobile phone off the bedside table and dialled 999. I was in such a state that I couldn't operate the phone menu to find my contacts directory and call a mate and this time the paranoid thought never entered my head that the police might show up (they never ever did). When the paramedics arrived they assessed me all the while listening to my tale of woe. I was advised I wasn't having a cardiac arrest I was having a panic attack. I was given advice on what to do should it happen again and told to make an appointment to see my GP which I did and she arranged for me to have cognitive behavioural counselling with a local therapist adding that this might take a while to set up.

Wednesday, 13 March, 2002

Five weeks had passed since I'd been discharged from hospital and during this time I'd learned the fine art of 'avoidance'. I'd had more panic attacks but these were always when I was on my own so I did everything in my power to try and avoid this which variously involved persuading friends to come and stay, going and staying with friends and of course getting a rental in which was starting to prove rather expensive and I explained all this to my therapist the afternoon I met her for the first time and she'd asked for a full disclosure of my lifestyle.

"Don't worry," she'd said, after we'd exchanged pleasantries and I'd sat down in her office. "I've heard it all before."

Just as well, I'd thought to myself though I did smile when she'd widened her eyes as I'd told her about the rentals and how it was actually true that sometimes men sought them out just for company... someone to talk to... an affectionate hug!

The principles of Cognitive Behavioural Therapy were outlined and I was told that I would have to commit to ten one-hour sessions every two weeks. During these talking sessions I would learn how to manage the problems that overwhelmed me by changing how I thought and behaved. It seemed like a good plan. I was willing to try anything and so I agreed to sign up for the course and as I did this my therapist commented that I kept looking at the clock on the wall (4:45pm) and asked me if time was also something that preyed on my mind. I laughed and told her that right now this was true because Chelsea were playing Tottenham Hotspur in exactly three hours and I was going to the game.

"Ah yes, you mentioned Chelsea," she replied. "Didn't they beat Spurs just the other day?"

"Yes. 4-0 at the Lane in the FA Cup."

"Lucky then."

"Ha, ha! Are you into football?" Briefly, a hope flickered into my mind that my therapist, a strikingly attractive woman of indeterminate age, might reply, "yes, but I've never been to a match, and I really like Chelsea... will you take me to a game?" But this instantly dissipated when she replied, "No, but my husband is."

"Who does he support?"

"Tottenham of course."

"Tell him he's never too old to change his team," I countered, slightly crestfallen.

My therapist laughed and bade me farewell. "Enjoy the game," she said, as I got up to leave.

*****

The Blues thrashed Spurs 4-0 with Jimmy Floyd Hasselbaink scoring a perfect hattrick (sequenced, right foot, header, left foot) and Frank Lampard rounding off the rout. The following week when I had my first full session with my therapist she'd asked me about the game and I'd described the atmosphere and the goals and the elation I'd felt. As the positivity about back-to-back 4-0 wins over Spurs tumbled from my lips she suggested I should write down my memories as expressive writing could benefit my situation. I told her about the article I'd written for the

'Chelsea Independent' a decade previously and also that I'd not written anything further because basically I spent all my free time getting wasted.

My 'homework' from this session was to sit down and write every day at the time when I would generally start to feel anxious about being alone, the trigger for my panic attacks. This would typically be around 9.30pm. This distraction technique proved to be a simple solution, and as the weeks passed and I had more sessions and did more writing (a couple of paragraphs at a time that I would write and re-write until I was happy with them) my mental health improved and the panic attacks became less frequent and severe. I had scarcely touched alcohol and not been near drugs since coming out of hospital, however I also hadn't spoken to anyone apart from my therapist about the extent of my problems and my family knew absolutely nothing. This was still a time when 'man-up' was what we men had to do in times of trouble. Anything else was seen as a sign of weakness which left you open to public ridicule.

During the summer of 2002 my therapy sessions came to an end. I was feeling much more at ease with myself and started traveling abroad a lot with work and although this was quite intense it kept me away from temptation and I continued with my writing. The World Cup was on in Japan so I wrote bits and pieces about that and when the football season finally ended I wrote about the places I visited with work. Paris, Milan, Munich, Prague, Budapest, Istanbul. I imagined Chelsea playing in the Champions League again and writing about exciting football trips abroad, but all Claudio Ranieri's team had managed to do of late was stumble into and rapidly out of the old UEFA Cup. Financially, the Club was unstable and teetering on the brink of insolvency, a reality check was needed; no, make that a blank cheque or a miracle, or both. Who knew that's the way things would map out at Stamford Bridge? Nobody!

Life for me was sadly more predictable and I succumbed once more to all the sinful temptations the world had to offer. Just one line of the devil's dandruff, a really small one... it won't do any harm. I know how to keep on top of things now. Big mistake! Chelsea may have been skint, but Roman Abramovich's billions would fix that. I was spiritually and morally bankrupt, for me cash wasn't the solution it only made matters worse and I was soon past caring especially as I now had a coping mechanism for the panic attacks that followed the drink and drug-fuelled binges that came all to easily to me again.

I had a wall calendar at home on which I planned every day for weeks and months ahead with obsessive precision. Football permitting (all Blues fixtures were calendarised), Sunday, Monday and Tuesday evenings were set aside for going to the gym and then writing. Chelsea qualifying for the Champions League in May 2003 and this being a catalyst for the Abramovich takeover a few weeks later had given me the idea for what would become my first book, 'Over Land And Sea', a travelogue-style account of the 2003/2004 season. On Wednesday's I would get booze and gear sorted for the weekend which in my world always started on a Thursday night as I regularly worked from home on Friday's. As a rule, even though I was living on my own, I never kept drink or drugs in the house beyond what I'd get through at the end of the week. Looking back, it seems ridiculous, but it's how I functioned and the granular detail of it all was my big secret and it remained so even after I met the lady I would eventually settle down and have a child with.

Saturday, 8 July, 2012

Fast-forward almost a decade and by now I was 51-years-old. I had a beautiful daughter, a loving partner, a nice home and I was writing more and more. Chelsea had not long since won the Champions League for the first time and were widely recognised as one of the elite clubs in world football. Life was good and my appetite for partying had waned. Certainly, my days of clubbing and staying up for nights on end were over however my inner demons were alive and well and ready to derail my normality train at the slightest opportunity... such as the evening I decided to take a very precise replica of the Champions League trophy, complete with engravings and blue and white ribbons, which was temporarily in my possession, on a tour of the hostelries in Cheam Village where I live. My partner and daughter were away for the weekend, it was 7pm, I'd just pop out for an hour or so. No harm in that. It would be a laugh. What could possibly go wrong?

A little over 10 miles from Stamford Bridge, Cheam is a Chelsea stronghold and word soon spread of the fantastic opportunity for selfies with the trophy and everywhere I went I was greeted as if I were Father Christmas. Everyone wanted to get in on the photo action. Santa has mince pies and sherry waiting for him at the breast of every chimney he descends, I was offered serial shots of the latest trendy drink, Jägermeister and something for the nose as well. By midnight, I was absolutely hammered and decided to go home. It's only half-a-mile from the centre of Cheam to my house but it was raining heavily and as I struggled along the road carrying the Champions League trophy I decided to shelter under the railway bridge on Station Way. Despite now only being 250-yards from home I sat down, embraced the trophy and waited for the rain to ease off. It didn't, so I stayed put and at some point I passed out.

The inclement weather must have kept people off the pavement and traffic off the road as I was undisturbed for several hours. I only came round when the drains under the railway bridge, unable to cope with the heavy rain, flash-flooded. As I opened my eyes, I saw that flood water had risen to cover my legs and was continuing to rise. I was soaking wet and shivering but still cradling the trophy! A surreal scene I'm sure. I got to my feet and staggered home and was violently sick shortly after.

The next day I renewed the vow I'd made and broken many times, "I'm never drinking again!" I was deeply ashamed of myself. I imagined how horrific the future might have been for my partner and daughter had I drowned or been sick and choked on my own vomit while I was lying under the railway bridge. To make matters worse if that could have been possible, the story would no doubt have made the papers. 'Chelsea fan drowns in bizarre Champions League trophy incident'. It was the sort of thing nobody would ever forget especially in Cheam Village as Station Way is the main thoroughfare. I imagined my partner walking my daughter to school and passing the scene of my demise every day and began to cry.

Shocked into sensibility, but maintaining a cloak of shameful secrecy, I knew I had to fill my time in such a way that my mind was distracted from thoughts of getting high. I started writing prolifically and began helping other people with their literary projects. I taught myself how to typeset books and design covers and created 'Gate 17' as a platform to showcase these new works. All of this was (and remains) extremely time-consuming, but in a good way. The whole process from ideation to publication of a book became my new addiction. A buzz without any harmful side-effects. Collaborating on projects to me is like a form of group therapy. Writing remains a hobby not a living. Of course I dream that one day I might achieve commercial success but that's not why I write and encourage others to write.

I'm 60-years-old now and the truth is I still haven't fully embraced sobriety but I do my best and I'm deeply sorry for all the hurt and upset my behaviour has caused and I'm also grateful to God that I have a roof over my head and food to eat and family and close friends who look out for me.

Since the railway bridge episode I've strayed off the straight and narrow a few times but with every year that passes it's less frequent and less far and I keep a photo in my wallet of my precious daughter and look at it often to remind me of my true purpose in life. I've had a few more health issues to contend with and struggled massively at times with the depression, anxiety and insomnia they caused. During the harsh winter lockdown of 2021 which followed a spell in hospital I couldn't sleep for weeks and the angst this caused drove me to the brink of insanity. I contemplated suicide. Fortunately, I sought out help from my GP and the local 'Uplift' mental health team who suggested I open-up to people I thought might be willing to listen. I shared my feelings of shame about past excesses and talked about my current anxieties. The Chelsea supporter community proved to be a tower of strength in this respect. I still have dark moments of shame, I'm not sure they will ever fully go away but now I can see a way forward and I've endeavoured to promote initiatives such as 'Over The Line', the Chelsea Supporters' Trust mental health education and support service in the hope that others struggling with psychological issues and/or life's obstacles might seek help and find someone to talk to about their problems.

Do I deserve to still be alive? Sometimes I question this. I often think of members of my family and dear friends who were taken from this life before their time and the unfairness of it all. The sadness associated with this can be overwhelming but I know this isn't unique to me. Bereavement affects everyone and grief can be reawakened at any time even many years after a loss.

I have many people to thank for their help and kindness in recent years and I try to do this often. This book provides me with the opportunity to recognise one person in particular to whom I believe I owe a huge debt of gratitude and that is Mark Meehan, founding father of the 'Big Stamford Bridge Sleepout', who published that first article I wrote all those years ago and in doing so altered the course of my personal history which in turn may well have saved my life.

"Thank you, Mr Meehan."

It's okay not to be okay, reach out for a chat anytime.
Twitter @gate17marco
Twitter @GetOvertheLine www.overtheline.uk
#MentalHealthMatters

GATE 17
THE COMPLETE COLLECTION
(SUMMER 2022)

CHELSEA

Over Land and Sea – Mark Worrall
Chelsea here, Chelsea There – Kelvin Barker, David Johnstone, Mark Worrall
Chelsea Football Fanzine – the best of cfcuk
One Man Went to Mow – Mark Worrall
Chelsea Chronicles (Five Volume Series) – Mark Worrall
Making History Not Reliving It –
Kelvin Barker, David Johnstone, Mark Worrall
Celery! Representing Chelsea in the 1980s – Kelvin Barker
Stuck On You, a year in the life of a Chelsea supporter – Walter Otton
Palpable Discord, a year of drama and dissent at Chelsea – Clayton Beerman
Rhyme and Treason – Carol Ann Wood
Eddie Mac Eddie Mac – Eddie McCreadie's Blue & White Army
The Italian Job, A Chelsea thriller starring Antonio Conte – Mark Worrall
Carefree! Chelsea Chants & Terrace Culture – Mark Worrall, Walter Otton
Diamonds, Dynamos and Devils – Tim Rolls
Arrivederci Antonio, The Italian Job (part two) – Mark Worrall
Where Were You When We Were Shocking? – Neil L. Smith
Chelsea, 100 Memorable Games – Chelsea Chadder
Bewitched, Bothered & Bewildered – Carol Ann Wood
Stamford Bridge Is Falling Down – Tim Rolls
Cult Fiction – Dean Mears
Chelsea, If Twitter Was Around When… – Chelsea Chadder
Blue Army – Vince Cooper
Liquidator 1969-70 A Chelsea Memoir – Mark Worrall
When Skies Are Grey, Super Frank, Chelsea And The Coronavirus Crisis – Mark Worrall
Tales Of The (Chelsea) Unexpected – David Johnstone & Neil L Smith
The Ultimate Unofficial Chelsea Quiz Book – Chelsea Chadder
Blue Days – Chris Wright
Let The Celery Decide – Walter Otton
Blue Hitmen – Paul Radcliffe
Sexton For God – Tim Rolls
Tales From The Shed – Edited by Mark Worrall
For Better Or Worse – Jason Gibbins
Come Along And Sing This Song – Johnny Neal's Blue And White Army

FICTION

Blue Murder, Chelsea Till I Die – Mark Worrall
The Wrong Outfit – Al Grogg
The Red Hand Gang – Walter Otton
Coming Clean – Christopher Morgan
This Damnation – Mark Worrall
Poppy – Walter Otton

NON FICTION

Roe2Ro – Walter Otton
Shorts – Walter Otton
England International Football Team Quiz & Trivia Book – George Cross

www.gate17books.co.uk

Printed in Great Britain
by Amazon